LOVE
& THINGS

By Xavier Echon

POEMS & INSPIRATIONAL WRITINGS

By Xavier Echon

Published by BookBaby

Manufactured in the United States of America

Cover Design: Josh Lau

Print ISBN: 978-1-66784-646-0
eBook ISBN: 978-1-66784-647-7

Contents

I

II

III

IV

V

VI

Love and Things is a love letter to the world. A compilation of spoken words transcribed and compiled from the left behind works of Xavier Echon, a boy who lived his life with a curious eye and generous heart. *Love and Things* teaches us to find love in the simplest of ways and weaves a narrative of resilience, courage, and beauty. These poems are Xavier's legacy, the words he left behind sketch the world that he saw; a passionate, beautiful life where socks fall in love with chopsticks and hearts break like birthday piñatas.

I Really Do This...

Pieces of Things

After my heart was broken like a
birthday piñata,
I stared at its contents,
surprised that there was so much,
for only one person.
Just pieces of
bubblegum compliments
that somehow lost its flavor,
chocolate-covered promises
that only melted in the heat
of things,
cherry-flavored "I love you's"
that will never be unwrapped
and enjoyed,
just pieces of things
I wanted you to save
for later.

Instead

So last night I had a dream, and in this dream my mind
took us back to when I met you and you met me for
the first time.
We relived past lives, yet each step backwards through
time began feeling like billions of years.
And I forgot everything that I wanted to tell you to the
point where I was too nervous to even introduce myself
to you.

See, we were both stars.
Billions of years ago when the universe was still young.
We formed the same constellations and together we
brightened the sky.
But you were always miles away from me.
So, I whispered messages on stardust, and I sent them
to you.
But by the time they got there, I died.

And then I was resurrected as a Greek who lived in Athens.
And you were a goddess who lived on Mount Olympus.
And every day I walked to the foot of the mountain hoping
you'd look down from the Pantheon, and noticed that the
constellations in my veins matched yours.
But I was just a mortal.

And I died worshiping a marble statue of you that barely
captured fractions of your beauty, and then I opened
my eyes, and I was Leonardo De Vinci, and you were
Mona Lisa.
And I thought maybe, just maybe, if I painted the comets
in your smile perfect enough, you'd remember me.
But when I finished my painting, you never came back.
And I died without ever seeing you again.

And then I came back again as a Hummingbird.
And every day I'd visit you while you watered your garden.
I would sing you songs sweeter than any orchestra could
ever play for you.
And I thought finally, you'd recognize me.
But one day, you moved away.
And the loneliness killed me.

And when I awoke, I was a piece of chalk.
And you were an eraser.
We were both owned by Albert Einstein.
I would write equations on the board.
You would fix all my mistakes.
We completed each other.
But when he died, so did we.

But I never gave up.
And I kept coming back to look for you.
I wore a name tag everywhere I went.
Thinking to myself maybe, just maybe, you were one
of the strangers that I passed by every day.
And seeing my name will help you to remember.
I drew arrows on pieces of cardboard that I would
hammer onto telephone poles.
They would point in the direction of my house.
And I prayed once, just once you'd follow them like
breadcrumbs and we'd find each other again.

I wrote hundreds of letters that I would put into these
glass bottles.
I would cast them out to random directions of the sea.
Hoping just once, just once, one would float to your feet
while you walked on the beach continents away.
And you'd read it and write me back.
But each time you never did, and I died.
Man, I died without ever finding you.
But even worse, I died right before
I got a chance to tell you.
It took me a billion years to say.

That's why today.
Maybe I'll hug you just a little too tight.
Or make it awkward if I stare at the stars in your
eyes for too long.
But it's only because I'm scared.
That one day I'm going to lose you.
And I'm going to have to find you all over again.
And let's be honest,
I do not want to spend another billion
years looking for you. I want to spend them with you,
Instead.

Rendezvous

I wonder
if the dream versions
of ourselves
still meet up in our dreams
every so often.
A subconscious rendezvous,
when both our beings
momentarily stop
shaping lives separate
from one another
to live out the promises
we failed to keep.

Queen of Hearts

So, one night I decided that I was going to write you
the perfect love poem.
A poem so incredibly crafted that you'd understand
just how much you mean to me.
The only problem though, is once I start to write about love,
It never seems to fully grasp everything I want it to mean.
I guess it just goes to show that love is more
than just words on a page, but nonetheless,
I still wanted to write you the perfect love poem.

Look, I'll be honest with you.
Love and I never really saw eye to eye.
In fact, the relationship between me and love is
like a game of hide and seek.
And if you didn't know, love is really good at hiding.
I searched and searched and ended up looking in
all the wrong places at all the right times.
And just when I decided I was going to give up,
I met you.

Look, I'll be honest.
I'm not a very sappy person.
But deep down, I always wanted to find love.
I want that, let's stay up all night and talk kind of love,
that let's make all the couples jealous kind of love,
that when I'm with you I want to pour out my heart kind of love,
that I love you so much I don't know where to start kind of love,
that God damn it hurts like crazy when we're apart kind of love,
that let's talk about our future plans kind of love,
that let's make inside jokes we only understand kind of love,
that I respect you kind of love, that don't worry babe
I'll protect you kind of love, that oh my goodness I'm so cheesy
whenever I text you, kind of love, I want love.
And all the good and bad that comes with it.
But more specifically, I want your love.
So just give me the chance to make you fall in love with me.

Let me be your Aladdin and take you around the world.
I'll show off the sunshine in your smile so that everyone
can feel the warmth of your "hellos".
And the entire world, can meet my entire world.
And I'll secretly learn words from every country and write
you a poem using every language ever spoken so that
whoever reads it, will know how much you mean to me.
So just give me the chance to make you fall in love with me.

Let me be your knight in shining armor.
Actually, no, I'd rather not be.
Instead, let me be your knight with dirty armor.
So, you know that I'll do all the hard work love requires.
Let my tarnish still be a symbol of how I'll never
give up on you.
No matter how many battles we have to go through.
So just give me the chance to make you fall in love with me.

Let me tell you what I think about you.
How I notice the diamonds in your eyes whenever you look at me.
That your laugh is more relaxing than listening to an ocean
on a summer's day.
Your voice is the greatest song ever composed.
You make me wonder if I'm sleeping.
Because I swear, you're the girl of my dreams.
You make me extremely nervous when you're around.
So nervous that you make my mouth play basketball.
As I stutter step through sentences that are meant to
make you think I'm not so much of a loser.
So just give me the chance to make you fall in love with me.

Just give me a day to sweep you off your feet.
Let's watch the sunrise and run our fingers through the sand.
Let's get lost in the crowds so all we know is each other.
Let's act like we're kids while love is still young.
Let me hold you close if the wind gets a little too cold
for your liking.
Let's live in the moment because I swear those last forever.
Let's make wishes on stars so I can secretly hope that you wish
to be together too.

I'm sorry if I'm trying way too hard to win you over.
But the world is a deck of cards that's been cut and shuffled
too many times.
So, what are the odds that I get dealt a Queen of Hearts
with the diamond eyes and a world full of spades and clubs?
I'll place all my bets on the table.
And expose myself to you so you know I have nothing to hide.
I'm sorry if this is so hard to understand.
But how can I explain being captivated by an angel?
You're the best thing I never knew I would need.
So, my love poem for you will probably never have an ending.
Because real love never ends.

So please,
If it is not too much trouble, just give me the chance
to fall in love with you.

Moonlight

On nights like this, when the
city lights look like fireflies ballroom
dancing with lightning bugs,
when women in shooting star dresses
linger in sea of night sky black tuxedos
just long enough to wish for forever,
and the wind is just a stray
Siren's song whispering,
"hold each other closer,"
I remember the night we first met.

Hello.
I know this is very upfront,
but I just wanted to be the
first to tell you that I couldn't
help but notice how your eyes,
brown lit beautiful,
made the skyline insecure,
that celestial-coated smile,
when you caught the world
staring a split second too long,
and I know you probably get this a lot,
but exactly how much heaven did
God use to make you?

You see I've noticed that lately
skyscrapers tend to look more
beautiful if draped in moonlight,
and moonlight tends to look more
beautiful if draped against you,
like a spectacular canvas,
you're a masterpiece of the universe,
let's paint the town red carpet amazing.

Life is just sweet rain drops of chaos,
In the heart of a city that swallowed
us whole and I just want to get lost
in the melancholy of it all,
If it means I can be next to you,
even if it's just for the night.
And did I mention,
the moonlight is draped against you just right.
I'm sorry,
I'm getting a little ahead of myself
so let me start over,

Hello.
You look gorgeous tonight,
with all the noise and bright lights maybe,
this city is just a club,
and darling,
when's the last time you really danced?
So, if you're up for it,
even if it's only tonight,
take my hand,
and I'll lead the way.

On the Topic of Death: Finding Life

So, I am taking this class called "Death and Dying" during the month of January 2016. When I tell people that this is the class I chose, 99.9% of the time I get the same follow up question: "So…what do you learn about in that class?" To which I respond with the truth: "We learn about the process of death…and dying."

Now, you are looking at your screen with the same curious/concerned look that most people give me after describing to them what exactly I learn in class. I do not blame you. In fact, I gave myself that same look when I registered for that class during my fall semester of Junior Year. I mean what was I thinking? Did I really want to come back from Christmas Break and talk about death for a month? I am an optimistic person, but I saw nothing beneficial about spending a precious month learning about grief, loss, sadness, and of course, dying.

Halfway through this month-long course, despite physically writing down the exact age I am going to die, how exactly I will die, and my own eulogy, I would recommend this type of course to anyone. Like myself at first, people are turned off by what the name of the class implies for the curriculum taught. Naturally, people do not want to learn about death. What people do not realize, however, is that this class is teaching people how to live. *I mean really, truly live.*

It came to me the day I watched *Tuesdays with Morrie* (great movie, better book) this was also the day I wrote down the age I was going to die. 88. So I finish the movie and look at my paper that I filled out and think 'What the hell… I'm twenty-one, which means, if my guess is correct, I only get sixty-seven more years to do exactly what I want to do.' Yes, that is a lot of time. But there is uncertainty in that eighty-eight. I could live longer maybe even for another decade but, in retrospect, I could have a much shorter life as well. There is too much uncertainty with life to give yourself a concrete age to when you think your story will end. We are dynamic beings so, by nature, the ability to predict the timeline of our lives is utterly impossible. *And that is when this beautiful revelation came to me.*

Look let us face it, sometimes we forget that our lives will one day end. It is inevitable. Society, especially modern society, makes the mistake of constantly urging us to live, while forgetting to remind us that we will die. It's given people, me included, this false sense of immortality and that we will always have time to live. We will always have time to chase our dreams. Then suddenly something goes wrong or old age creeps up on us and we are left feeling unfulfilled or even cheated out of what we thought was a promise of getting to really live. This "Death and Dying" course, which I was so sure was going to dampen my spirits, taught me one of the most important lessons I already knew: *Live before you die.*

I know most of you will not get the chance to take a class like this. So, I will give you what you should take away. Live life to the very fullest because one day, a day you do not know, everything will come to an abrupt halt. I want to tell people now, especially people like me who are fresh into their twenties working towards an undergraduate degree or profession, that life is too short to not study what you want, or be what you want to be, or do what you want to do. You may ask: "Where do I even start?"

Realize now that life is a finite thing, while you still have the chance to control your destiny. Do not put it off until tomorrow and do not give anything less than your best. There are no second chances when it comes to living so make sure that you give everything you've got into this one life. Go to the gym and get that body that you promised yourself three summers ago. Or eat what you want, screw that diet. Chase that job people said would be too risky to make a living off. Go to that school that offered you a scholarship but is thousands of miles away from everything you know. Make that YouTube account and fill it with all the videos you think will make you famous. Write that book. Forgive that person. Tell her how you feel. Tell him how you feel. Help others. Travel the world. Meet people. Smile often. Say I love you. Take risks. Fail. Succeed. Find peace. Believe in the good. Be humble. Work your ass off. Search for happiness. Chase dreams.

Do not keep telling yourself that tomorrow is the day that you will turn your life around. Start today. Please, start today. Because one day we are all going to wake up and realize that there are not many tomorrows left. And I do not know about you, but when that day comes for me, I want to smile to myself and say I gave it my best shot. I want to tell myself that I lived every day in hopes of fulfilling my potential. That I did not waste one, single second on something I did not honestly think was important.

So, in short, I am now a twenty-one-year-old guy that just had the deepest revelation at 12:06 AM. I think some self-care is in order so tomorrow I think I will play basketball and lift weights even though I'm supposed to have a rest day. Aware of my own mortality I am going to now get everything I can out of life while I am still capable. I hope anyone who reads this will do the same.

Dear Basketball

I want to keep this as short as possible.
You've given me many things to be grateful for:
lasting friendships and relationships,
millions of memories, respect,
and self-confidence to name a few.
You also taught me how to dedicate myself
to something and obsess over the single desire
to simply be better than I was each day.
You pushed me and pushed my will until
I became the man I am today.
Don't get me wrong;
I was never the best player (or the tallest),
but I worked hard for you.
Because isn't that what you do for
someone or something that you love?
When the doctors told me that my playing
days were over,
I expected to feel a piece of me disappear.
For the most part, I got what I expected,
and it was hard to picture not competing,
battling, and running with other athletes.
But it turns out I felt more grateful,
because ironically what I thought was a
basketball injury turned out to be
another gift for me: my life.
Without you, I would've never found
the cancer in my leg as early as I did.
I never would've prepared for chemo
with a high chance of recovery.

You're giving me a fighting chance,
and I'll make the most of it.
And although it's time to hang up
the competitive sneakers,
I'll still be around to shoot hoops
now and again or teach others.
Because let's face it,
you don't really stay away from what you love.
Thanks, basketball.
S/O to the beautiful game!
With love,
X

Snowfall

If you ever fall in love,
my only wish is that you fall
like how snow meets the
ground floor the first time.
Slowly.
I hope you get lost in the
blizzard of snowflake
moments that results when
two lives unexpectedly
fit together.
And if you get there,
I hope you melt
in the heat of all that passion.
But do so slowly.
Softly.
As if,
you have forever to spare.

Simplicity

There are those days,
when life becomes the perfect cocktail
mix of dysfunction and chaos, when
stress piggyback rides on my shoulders
as a constant reminder of how much weight
a bad day really carries,
I have those days.
And on these particular days, when life
seems more like a field of landmines than
a field of lemons for life's lemonade
of optimism, I wish I kept memories in
mason jars.
Memories that would coat my hippocampus
with the sweet scent of, "Remember when," and
"Those were the days back then," to remind me
that life isn't always a back against the wall
brawl to victory.

I'd keep a jar of what you look like first thing in
the morning.
Because organic is in, and isn't beauty truly beauty,
if it's as natural as God intended?
And in my opinion, 10 AM sunshine is the only
foundation you really need.
And there's just something about how you use
sleep as eyeliner that makes me fall in love every day.
Look,
I apologize in advance that oftentimes,
I sound like a broken record when it comes to talking
about you.
But personally. . . personally, I think saying you are
gorgeous is something that should always be on replay.

I'd keep a jar of every spontaneous adventure.
Of every forearm-sized calzone and burrito,
every single second when we sidelined responsibility.
I'd download the laughs we shared, and copy & paste
the smiles so that when life is more hardship than joy,
we would always have that moment when we thought
we really could live forever off of love.

I'd keep a jar of every time I played "Love Yours"
so that when the demons in my heart loosened my will,
the lyrics were there to show me that there will always
be beauty in my struggles, just pearl-coated bullets of
truth to vanquish the doubt.

I'd keep a jar of my ambition to remind myself that
I still have dreams to chase, and I still have an
unfinished picture of myself I want to paint for others.
That desire for success that pushes me to fight for every
inch life gives me.

I'd keep
a jar of that final swish.
A jar of that Italian pasta.
A jar of driving with all the windows down.
A jar of all the pieces of Heaven
I found on Earth.
One for waiting at the airport.
One for every hug.
A jar for all the times I heard
"I love you."
"I'll never give up on you."
"You saved me."
"I miss you."
"Fight for me."
"Fight for you."
"You inspire me."
"Thank you."
"I'm yours."
"I need you."

To remind me,
that the summation of a person is less what they
accomplish for themselves, but more so what they
do to touch the life of another person.

And as for the last jar,
I'd keep it for what it felt like to lose everything.
The moment where one diagnosis changed it all.
I'd fill it to the brim with all the tears and all the
fear, to remind myself I'm human and that
imperfection is the real beauty in the grand
scheme of things.
That weakness is the only way to learn to be strong.
And that sometimes you must break in order to one
day be indestructible.

I'll keep this jar to recount the greatest story ever told.
About how cancer ravaged my body but never dented
my soul.
I'd make sure to keep this one mason jar just as safe.
To remind me,
On those days,
How much the other jars really mean.

To Whom It May Apply

I want you to think about your dreams, not the dreams your
parents have for you, or the dreams your friends have for
you, but the dreams that you have always had for you.
And I want you to picture, whether it be months or
years from now, fulfilling all those dreams and what your
life looks like.

Maybe you're a producer, maybe you're a business owner,
maybe you got that body, made those friends you never had,
got that relationship you were always jealous of;
picture something you really want in this life and hold it.
How happy does that make you feel?

Now I'm going to let you guys in on a secret everyone knows.
The only way to find any type of success in this world is to
make the concerted effort to risk what feels comfortable to you.
That means getting used to the idea that the road to your dreams
and all the success will rarely ever be a comfortable path.
In fact, you need to accept the fact that there will be a lot of
"No's" before you hear your first "Yes", or you will reach
multiple dead ends and go through multiple failures before
something works once in your favor. It will be hard,
and life will constantly punch you in the mouth
and dare you to get back up. It will punch you square
in the jaw and tell you that your dreams are too far-fetched,
too risky, utterly unreachable, not practical, and you'll be there,
on your back looking up at life. And life won't offer a hand
to help you up, it won't! You'll be there in your own blood,
sweat, and tears forced between choosing the life that you
want and a life that is easy.

I'm here to tell you today that if you really want the life
you dreamed of, you can't half ass it and expect the full results.
You have got to fully commit to the process.
Greatness requires everything from you, dreams require
maximum effort. Look I get it there will be days when
you don't want to grind, don't want to get out of bed,
don't want to go to that interview, question if the dream
is worth all the sacrifice, all the obstacles.
Listen to me, if it was easy to get up every day and lift weights,
easy to face adversity, if it was easy to beat the odds,
easy to pass those classes, easy to say you love someone,
then everyone would do it.

The only difference is successful people are the people
who see how difficult the road is, take the punches in the mouth,
get up, look life right in the eyes, and say,
"I dare you to make me stop chasing my dreams.
I dare you to tell me I can't do something."
And they keep moving forward, even if they have to crawl for
each inch, even if it takes twice as long, even if they don't quite
see the end game, no matter the risk, they keep moving forward.

Look, at twenty-one, in the prime of my college career,
educational and athletic success, I was diagnosed with cancer.
For a while, I didn't know where the road was anymore.
For a while, I mentally checked out. There were times were
I doubted that I could even come back from it. But I realized
that I could either spend seven months feeling sorry for myself
or I could spend seven months fighting each day for what I
pictured for myself in the future. And I'm not here to make you
pity me or feel sorry for me but to tell you that sometimes
it's just going to be unfair!

Sometimes you'll have to take an extra job, sometimes you'll
have to stay up an extra two hours to understand something
it takes thirty minutes for other people to understand.
You might get sick and have to leave school.
You might not have the privilege, but you can have the heart
and you can have the will. So, outwork the privilege and
outwork the talent. The world isn't going to stop and wait
for you to get everything back so if you find yourself on
the ground you have to get right back into the fight.
Dreams only manifest themselves as tangible things
when you fight for them. You have to hold hope that each day
your dream is that much closer.

People will say no, people you love will leave,
people will secretly want you to fail, but don't you dare go
quietly into the night. Don't look back and wonder why you
settled and never at least tried. Put your head down,
find the people that support you, and push as hard as you can
for as long as you can until you look up and all you can say is,
"I made it, I did this."
And yes, it's going to hurt, you're going to get tired,
you're going to feel pain, but the pain is how you learn,
and learning is how you grow, growing is how you face adversity,
and facing adversity is how you become successful.

Just In Case

Just in case you start to feel like we are
growing up too fast, on those days where you
wish you could paper airplane us back to a time
that was a lot more simple and even more reckless.

Just in case,
I want to remind you, that a piece of me
will always be a mix of Matinee movie tickets,
Bart passes, missed curfews, cheap ramen,
photo booth pictures, matching bracelets,
and monthiversary letters.
And whatever product of my will I become,
I'll always just be this boy who really liked this girl
and thought she was all he would ever need.

Just in case life takes me half the world away,
I will bottle up a sound bite of your laugh to
take with me.
Let the vibrations replay in my head whenever
I opened it, so I always remember why
I chased my dreams.
And I will send you a picture of every coffee shop
I go to just so I wouldn't have to spend a morning
without you.

Just in case you start to feel ugly, when it seems
like everyone is just a floodlight exposing
your insecurities,
I will remind you that I've never met another
person who has the audacity to be beautiful even
if the world around her says she isn't.

Just in case,
I will say your smile could bring the world to
its knees.
Do not forget this.
You are violin and every step you take is a
musical masterpiece.
And just in case you haven't laughed today,
did you know after a tough day at work,
the dog said "man, today was ruff."

Just in case the phrase "I love you"
becomes too overused,
I will super glue different words together to
remind you how I feel,
Just in case, I will change "I love you" for you.
To: "I ordered us dinner",
"Take one of my sweatshirts with you",
or maybe,
"I know this is random, but I really miss you."
To: "You really brighten up the room",
"I made you soup because you haven't eaten since noon",
"Yeah I'll watch your shows with you too",
"Don't worry I'll drive you to whatever you have to do",
and even,
"I got you this record because it reminded me of you."

Just in case we get too busy,
Just in case life gets in the way,
Just in case things get difficult,
Just in case you really need me to say the right thing
this time,
I would say that every second
I invested into you has been worth it.
And if the only thing it costs to be around you is a
lifetime of seconds, I'd call that a steal.

Just in case,
I'll keep a copy of this behind the frame of your
favorite picture of us, and when you ask why
I kept it there all these years,
I'll look you in the eyes and say that sometimes
seeing what I say can mean just as much as hearing it.
And after you breathe all the good things about us back in,
I'd hide this again,
Just in case.

Sunlight

While your roots
are still stretching,
anchoring you
to the extreme conditions
of everyday life,
think carefully
before comparing someone,
you love to the sun.
Although nothing is more
romantic, there is nothing more
dangerous than naming the center
of your universe after someone,
other than you.
Think carefully.
Because if that same sun
decided to shine somewhere else one day,
Would you still be able to grow?

Heaven Brew

And if one day we find ourselves in some coffee shop across
the country, I hope that your laugh is still the same unique
brew it was all those years ago. I think the recipe was half
a cup of corny jokes, three-fourths of a cup of adventure,
and a spoonful of Snapple cap fun facts lightly shaken for
three minutes to your favorite song. Trust me, it's easy to
remember. I even came up with a name for it.

I called it "Heaven."

Anyways, I pray that life continued to be kind to you
in the two years since we last spoke. So kind, in fact,
that if you showed me the jigsaw puzzle known as
your everyday life, I'd still see some of the pieces
I helped put there. Things I wanted you to show off to
the world because they were worth the attention.

Truthfully, I'd probably only let myself talk to you for
ten minutes. I'd ask about your new job, if you like living
in this strange place, and if you still think donuts are
basically dessert bagels. Which they aren't. I'd ask
enough to make me want to run into you again one day.
But stop right before I started to miss you too much.
Your laugh is heaven.
But is heaven still heaven after going through hell?

So, if we do ever find ourselves in a coffee shop,
across the country, living a different life than the one
I thought we would be living. . . which is just a more
poetic way of saying "together," I hope things are well.
And when I tell you about what I'm doing,
what I've seen, and who I've loved since we last spoke,
I hope you still see some of the best pieces you added
to my life puzzle too. I imagine that you'd be happy to
know that parts of what made me a man started with
you. Then maybe we'd have another brew.
Heaven flavor of course.

Before we go our separate ways,
I'd give you a quick hug and hope that maybe I'd
see you around again. Odds are we won't.
It's a large city. But if you really think about it,
it's an even larger world.

And yet at one point in time, years before some
coffee shop across the country with lives that
were just jigsaw puzzles that we all spent
eternities on, when the chances were just as
slim as they were now, against all odds,
we found each other.
And isn't that enough to be happy about?

The story ends when we both disappear into different
spectrums of this concrete jungle. Just two fish in a
sea of winter coats, beanies, and regular cups of coffee.
At that point, I'd remember all the good times.
When our stories had each other as a main character.
When life seemed a lot easier to understand because
we had each other to figure it out with.
When hands were easier to hold than grudges.
And when heaven was just one laugh away,
I'd admit to myself that I miss you.

And I'd keep on walking.

Eight Things I Learned from Having Cancer

For a few months now, I've been playing with the idea of writing something about my journey with cancer. The problem, however, is writing something that doesn't come off as this obligatory recap of what can be considered the wildest year and half of my life.

I want this to resonate with you. And I know that won't happen if you get lost in the narrative.

I also personally think that this is not the time for sob stories about losing almost everything and then finishing it up with the motivational "But I'm coming back better than ever" bit. I'll tell that story when the time is right, but before we all get caught up in the drama of my journey, I want to tell you the important stuff first. I want to tell you what important things I learned from having to go through cancer.

A lot of the things on this list might make you think:

Duh, of course these things are important things to remember in life.

You're not wrong, but at the same time, do you know why you're not?

DISCLAIMER: I'm only twenty-two, so you can fairly say that it seems strange to take some life advice from someone who has yet to experience any life.

These are in no particular order, I just listed them as I went. So, if you're interested, curious, or down, here you go:

1. Learn the importance of self-reliance.

Before I go on, I don't mean you should shut out the world,
push everyone away, and **always** deal with things alone.
Truthfully, the whole "lone wolf" thing is not the most practical
way of handling adversities you come across.

What I mean is developing self-reliance so that you
understand that if things go wrong and it really comes down to it,
you can trust yourself to get through tough situations on your own.
I found that developing this skill helps me to really appreciate
when others offer their love and support because it becomes
something I can appreciate and cherish rather than blindly
cling onto.

Don't get me wrong; there will be people in your
life who will never complain about being your rock.
But if for some reason that rock isn't there,
you don't panic because your foundation is strong too.

2. Focus on what you can control.

One of the most important things that any doctor, oncologist,
surgeon, or nurse ever told me during this experience was that
when it came to cancer, I only had control over 10 percent
of what happens. That ten percent included if I was eating right,
staying physically active, taking the medication(s), etc.
The other ninety percent involves whether the treatment works.

Life, in general, works on a similar premise.
There will never be a time where you always have control over everything.
It's a waste of time to try. It will just lead you to being frustrated,
unhappy, and bitter.

You will find that life is more enjoyable, and the rewards
are much more satisfying if you just worry about
the things that fall under your control.

You can't make someone love you, but you can be the
best version of yourself and attract someone who will
choose to love you. You can't control if you get hired for
your dream job, but you can control the steps you have to
take to have the best chance. You can't control if you wake up
tomorrow, but you can control whether you make the most out
of each second you get.

Don't burden yourself with things you don't have any say in.
Worry about what you can do, and the rest will fall into place.

3. Make time for what/who you love.
Simply put, a lot of the things we all do in life are things we don't
necessarily enjoy. On top of that, it seems like there isn't enough
time to do all the stuff we don't even want to do in the first place.

During chemo, I was in this constant grind of doing things I really
hated doing. It really made me appreciate the times where I could
let go of the routine and workout, be with my friends,
or go outside the house.

No one can go 110 percent every second of the day.
Put some time aside every day to do things that you love doing
and to spend it with people that are important to you.

Build your passions and build your relationships. They are just as
important as grinding hard every day.

4. Commit to your goals and start them.
Like everyone else, you have those dreams and aspirations that
are in your head at night while you're in bed staring at the ceiling.

Don't let imaging and wishing for those things be enough for you.

Make goals you are passionate about, plan, and start them.
You never know where you'll end up or the opportunities you'll
have if you work toward what you're passionate about.

Try new things and take up new hobbies. Why wonder what could
have been when you could just see for yourself?

Life is too short and unexpected to not put yourself
on a path to things that will make you happy.
Having cancer put that into perspective for me.
If you want it, go get it.

5. *You are more powerful than you think.*
One thing I got a lot of over the course of this journey was:

"X, you are the strongest person I know."

Naturally, the statement always made me feel good. But the truth is
anyone can do what I did, and everyone has the same strength that I have.

**Honestly, I never knew how strong I was until my back was against
the wall and cancer forced the strength out of me.**

You have that will too; it's just a matter of being able to draw it
out of you when you want it. I wasn't born with an extraordinary
amount of willpower; I just went through enough to be able to
bring out a large amount when I really needed it.

You have the ability to endure things that you think
are impossible to overcome. The key is to let go of all the
fear and uncertainty that comes with any obstacle and
trust your instincts to take over for you. Don't overthink and
overanalyze it.

Tell yourself the plan and get there no matter what.

6. *Don't be afraid to reach out to people.*

No, I'm not going back on what I said about self-reliance.

Probably the hardest part of this whole experience was the mental toll that cancer and chemo had on me. There were times where it was very lonely and after a long enough time that isolation started getting to my head. Simple texts to my friends or planning to see them when I was healthy was enough to counteract all those negative feelings.

You shouldn't be afraid to tell people when you need them, especially if they are important people in your life. Yes, you could get through things on your own if you really needed to, but having other people around can take a lot of pressure off your shoulders.

And this also implies that you must be the one to reach out. As far as I know, people can't read minds. They won't know you need them if you stay silent.

7. *Enjoy the little things.*

When you go through something difficult, you become more aware of moments when you are genuinely happy. Often, they are moments you normally wouldn't pay any mind to.

When I first got diagnosed, a friend from high school told me to always look for the silver lining. I took that as trying to see the parts of my day that made me happy during a scary and uncertain time in my life.

If those little things were enough to get me through a situation most people can't even imagine being in, think of how much better it would make a regular day in your life.

Appreciate the beauty in something so simple.

8. Don't underestimate the power of time.

A year ago, I was this kid who was diagnosed with cancer and
had no idea what the hell was going to happen to me. I had just
made the decision to amputate my leg, and I had no idea how
I would make that work when it came to readjusting to everyday life.

Fast forward to today, and I'm on a new treatment that looks
very promising, and I have the physical ability to jog with a fake leg.
I no longer must isolate myself from the world, and I'm planning
to come back to school in the fall.

I know that getting here was a cumulation of those 365 days
where I slowly climbed my way back with nothing more
than an idea of what I wanted to be.

Life, in general, is very similar. There will be situations
that seem daunting when you first undertake them.
But no situation is permanent, and there are always little
things you can do to influence where you'll go.

Not every situation will be solved in a few days or weeks.
Few meaningful things you accomplish in life will ever happen
that quickly.

A year ago, if you told me I would eventually be this healthy,
I wouldn't believe you.
But here I am.

Homebound

And I hope you find happiness,
at the edge of the world,
where the sun
kisses the ocean,
Goodnight.

Awhile

That's what I tell people.
It's been awhile since I've seen you,
It's been awhile since I've spoken to you,
It's been awhile since I've loved you.
Of course,
one of those statements is a lie, but yeah. . .
It's been a while.

You know truthfully,
I hate the word "awhile"
because that's how long people say it'll
take to get over you.
It's just a one-word phrase for an uncertain,
but lengthy amount of time of loving
someone who doesn't love me back.

Let me put that into perspective,
that's an "awhile's worth" of milestones
I wish I could share with you.
An "awhile's worth" of moments that would
be exponentially better if you were with me.
An "awhile's worth" of time that nowadays
I just don't have to spare.
An "awhile's worth" of convincing myself
that I have to not care.

Again. . .
These days I hate when people say it'll take
a while to not feel this way about you.
And I hate it even more because
I know they're right.
When you left,
I lost a special piece of myself.
The piece that was most precious to me.
And they say it'll take awhile to find it if
I even find it at all.
They say it's going to take awhile to not
want to pick up the phone and say,
"Hey, it's been awhile. . . but I miss you, so
I thought I'd call."

And people have been saying I've been
different for awhile, but I guess that's been
the point of things for awhile.
Maybe deep down I want people to stop and
admire me even for a little while.
While you look back and regret not sticking
with me for a little while longer.
And I know I've said this for awhile but,
It seems like my mind has been running
for miles.

You know, it's been rough for awhile
while it looks easy for you all the while,
while we haven't been together in awhile
I still know pieces of heaven are stuck in your
smile.
And it's definitely taken me awhile, but I see
why people's albums go platinum after being
heartbroken for awhile.
And let me tell you the words just flow for a
good while these days.
And I hate that too, because awhile back I
would've loved to have so many words to
make a piece about you.

But in retrospect,
"Awhile" might not be as bad as
I make it out to be.
While it could mean years. . .
It could also mean tomorrow.

Honestly "Awhile" is a beautiful concept.
After all, what's more beautiful than
something that can't truly be defined?
I imagine that's why
I love you.

You're an awhile that I wished would stay
for a long while just a little while longer.
So, I'll keep waiting awhile.
While keeping an eye out for my next awhile.
Maybe it'll be you, or maybe it'll someone
else who will one day lovingly say to me,
"You sure kept me waiting awhile."
Or,
"I hope you stay awhile."
Perhaps my next awhile will be the kind of
awhile that's "forever awhile. . ."
And that thought alone, makes waiting awhile. . .
Very worthwhile.

Wondering

And I wish I could take you to all the interesting
places this world has to offer, just so I could hear
you laugh in all of them,

Wondering,

If falling in love is just a firefly dancing on your
skin. I'd take you to Paris in the rain just to
watch how quickly rain free falls from the sky
just to get a closer look at you. And I wouldn't
blame them, because I'd fall a million times for
you too. And sixty years from then, we'd be
eating at our favorite restaurant and between
spoonfuls of clam chowder you would tell me
about hummingbirds and outer space, and I'd sit there,

Wondering,

How after all this time, someone can still be infinite.
Our pockets are not filled with as much time as they
used to be, the story is drawing to a close, and we're
both wondering when the credits will start rolling,
but I can say, while wondering how it all led up to
this moment, that if our life together was a movie,
I'd get lost in its reruns.

Balloons

Tell them you are a balloon,
then they will love you tightly.
They will not shy away
from the heartstring you offer,
they will grasp at it,
as if desperate to hold onto your hellos.
They will love you tightly,
because you are a balloon.
And they know,
once they let go,
you'll never look back.

To The Pencil:
A Love Letter from a Classroom Desk

We met in August.
Homeroom.
It sounds crazy, but the minute you
were introduced to me,
I couldn't help but think that we've
met before as if cut from the same
exact tree. You were this gold
coated reminder of something
I couldn't quite wrap my mind around,
but what I could understand was that
you felt like a home far away from here.
Still, they told me not to grow too fond of you,
because come next year,
you wouldn't be around anymore.

We were both too stoic to ever speak

but I'd watch you spill all your
contents onto notebooks, papers,
and love letters. From arithmetic and
Ancient Greece to sketches of
sunflowers, for five days a week.
8 a.m. to 3 p.m. became my favorite time,
fascinated by all the knowledge you've
kept hidden in your spine.
I don't have much to offer you.
I don't have an infinite well of knowledge
to share with you when the days turn dry.

But I can be there to support you,
to make sure you always have a place
to rest when you are tired from
writing out your life for me.
You're so quick to rub out your mistakes,
but it's okay to me if you're not always right.
I'm not perfect either.
And I've noticed how sharp you get,
and I promise I can hold your world
up for you, so you never have to be
self-conscious of your ideas leaving holes
in anything you touch.

But that quality is twofold,

I know. . .

That you break easier the sharper you get,
so I will promise to cradle you until you
are whole again.
It's been months since we met, so I think
it's safe to give you a small piece of advice:
Always remember, never let that two that's
tattooed to your spine define you.
You've always been number one to me.

And it's been hard to watch you these days.

You're a lot weaker now and all the ideas
I've grown so attached to watching have
made you a lot smaller than I remember.
I wish you'd stop, but I love you too much
to make you give up the only thing you've
ever been passionate about.

I can see why the others said not
to grow too fond of you.
But loving you is something I'd never erase.
I know you'll have to move on from here,
and I'll always stay in this same place.
But I know you'll keep writing out your life.
Trying to make sense of things is exactly
what you were made to do.

But I hope,

If it's not too much trouble,

you'd etch something into my hands,

to always remind me,

of you.

To The Classroom Desk:
A Love Letter from a Pencil

We met in Homeroom.
August.
When they laid me onto your surface?
I wanted to ask if you were as scared
as I was. If you feared that the intensity
of the spark between us would ignite
our lumber bodies until we were
nothing but ash.

It was only August. . .
But I prayed that this year wouldn't
pass by so fast.
I had just met you. . .
But I swear, behind your polish finish
I recognized you from some different
life away from here.
And it's okay that you're not much
of a talker, I have so much to say,
and I love that you'll listen to all of it.
I'd ramble on about Cleopatra,
windmills, and the difference
between rivers and creeks,
from 8:00 a.m. to 3:00 p.m.,
five days a week. And after each lead
encased thought sank onto each line,
I would feel you shake,
as if you were able to make sense
of what went on in my mind.
So, I sketched you sunflowers hoping
they would brighten your day.

If you let me,
I could write that I love you
in every kind of way.
I know it's not easy being around me,
some days I seem dull, but on others,
I get too sharp for my own good.
I break easily, but you held me close
until I could speak again.
I made so many mistakes,
but you would always give
me the chance to make it right.

But I have started to notice,
when I take breaks to nap on your
shoulder, that you seem a lot sadder,
from noticing that I'm much older.
You still let me write and listen
all the same, I think I'll always
love you, even though here is
where you must remain.
They always said I was number two,
so, thank you for making me feel deserving,
of the number one spot to match with
my gold coating. When I leave,
I'll write about everything that I wish
we could be, but I hope,
If it's not too much trouble,
I can etch something onto your hands,
to always remind you,
of me.

To The Desk:
A Love Letter from a Pencil #2
By: Heidi Lahl

I saw you in September.
I traveled from desk to desk,
insecure of my identity and
lost in the shuffle.
Until one day, my spine felt your
grain for the first time.
The moment I was placed I knew
that I was home, I rolled over the
edges and did that familiar beat that
I knew we would both remember.

We never spoke, all those years ago,
but I hope you know that every
love letter and every sunflower
was meant for you.
I wanted to scratch my name
into your existence.
I wanted to tell you my world
and hope you would still love
me the same.
I always thought we were cut from the
same tree, is that so insane?
I remember laying back and you supporting
my spine as I imagined all the worlds
I was going to create.
You would creak from time to time,
and you always seemed to apologize
for not being quiet.
Those were the moments I knew I loved you,
the ones where I was held but not held down,
the moments where your vulnerability was
exposed even though you tried to hide it.

We are both cut from the same tree,
but I have been dwindled down to where
I may snap at any time.
You are strong and sturdy,
and I worry that there will be a point where
I will break, and you will remain.
But the reassurance of your creak always gave
me the courage to still create.

But these are all memories that seem to be erased.
You are not the same as you were all those years ago.
What I thought was home has been cluttered with
other affections.
You begged me to etch my life into your hands,
but I was too embarrassed to try.

Ever since the last day that I saw you,
I have tried to write my way back to you.
I have created theories and theorems,
and every classroom I entered,
I tried to catch a glimpse of you.
I dreamed of the day where I could finally
write on your surface all the things that
I had dreamed but now that I am here,
I see that there is no room for me.
You have drawings of planets and hearts with initials.
There is no space for my reflections,
you did not wait for my dreams.

It seems like you have rotted somewhere deep
where I cannot see, the home that I once had seems
dark and musty now, your grain no longer feels the same.
The scribbles of affection on your surface can never be unseen.
And if I wrote something now, would you even weep
when it faded on your grain?

Instinct

They told me birds fly
south for the winter.
That they were smart to
chase the sun when this
part of the world glazed over.
But I asked myself,
are they smart for chasing the sun?
Or,
are they fools for thinking
it could never
be as beautiful here?

To A Steering Wheel:
A Love Letter from a Pillow

They told me I was foolish for falling
in love with you, that you moved
through life too quickly for
someone that stays in bed all day.
That you are always on the go,
and more often than not,
I come across as perpetually lazy. . .

They said all you'd do is drive me crazy.
But I can't help but love you,
and it has nothing to do with your sporty
build or the fact you're the most popular
model in town these days.

I love you for your leadership.
Just a spherical, leather dressed shepherd,
wherever you turn everything seems to
follow suit.
You're not afraid to raise your voice if it
means you'll protect things from the
scratches and dents the world will
bombard you with.

I can't help but love you,
even if you sometimes get lost along
the way, even if you always seem to
work alone, everyone trusts you to
guide them home.

We rarely get to speak,
But I think we're a perfect match.
As great as you are,
I've seen you run on empty
when you forget to take breaks.
You're stiff and awkwardly shaped,
but I can mold myself in any way
that's comfortable for you.

The road you travel is bumpy,
and I've been told I cushion things
very well.
On most occasions, you'll blindly
measure your life in miles, from
point A to point B is all you
seem to care about sometimes.
I love you for your motivation,
but I can show you there's nothing
wrong with being idle.
I can teach that engine inside you
to appreciate the calm.
Yes, the destination is important,
but there's something to
be said about the journey there as well.

I know you'll read this and have no
idea what it means, but trust me,
I've spent years listening to dreams.
And I could do that for you too.
So please unlock yourself and be
open to what we can be, then we can
go to all the places you've always
wanted to see, and when you get tired,
I'll be your passenger, and you can
lay your head on me.

To A Staple:
A Love Letter from a Paperclip

I know it's wrong of me to write you,
that I'm putting us both in danger for
nothing more than the selfish fact that
I love you.
After all, our families have never
gotten along for as long as I can remember.
Generations of fighting over who can better
hold the world together.

I met you by mistake.
But then again,
Isn't that just a more pessimistic way of
saying I met you exactly at the right time?
But I didn't know how to approach you.
So I just watched you from afar.
I watched how tightly you held onto
things, as if they were the last moments
you had left in this world.
And I think that's when I knew,
I was in love.

You'd do anything to keep things
together even contort your bridge shaped
body to make sure they could never
escape your embrace.
I do that too. . .
But with you it's different.
Because whenever they force you to let
go everyone can still see the holes in
the lives you leave behind.

And that's when I knew,
If I ever made you mine,
I'd never let you go.
And perhaps loving you is a mistake.
But then again,
Isn't that just a more pessimistic way
of saying I know it'll be difficult
but I'll love you regardless?

You and that silver coated smile mixed
with pieces of stardust.
Our families would never approve,
but my heart has already fixed you up
a room so, feel free to latch onto it
in whichever way feels like home.
And then I will coil my arms around you,
and hold you tightly,
as if the entire world,
was watching.

To a Chopstick:
A Love Letter from a Sock

My neighborhood is a paradox.
The streets are cluttered with high rises
and new tenants are moving in by the boxful.
They swear their residency is temporary,
that once they find employment, mend their
damaged pieces, and remember what it's like
to be remembered, they'd move away.
Most never do.
By definition it should be a bustling metropolis,
but on most days, this city seems satisfied
sitting in its silence.

I remember the day you moved in.
You lived in the building called "Kitchen"
and I was right across the street in the one
called "Goodwill."
Your slender build perplexed me.
I thought someone had to have picked you
up off the street, and through some cruel
twist of fate discarded you here.
You were small and fragile, and I figured
this place would splinter you.
That you would snap under the weight
of the unreasonable dreams that
get lost up here.

But I always thought fondly of you.
And I was certain that for someone, you'd
make a great catch.
And then I fell in love, when I learned that,
like me, you also lost your match.
I wanted to ask you if ever felt bitter,
If you ever cursed the world under your
breath like I did, for having your existence
hinged on a partner that disappeared one
morning that didn't even have the decency
to leave a note scribbled with apologies.

I watched and waited. . .
wondering if you wanted to sock fate in the
chest for things you had no say in.
But you just lied there, content with how the
world had carved your life.
You're on the bottom floor and the
other tenants pile on you until I can barely
make you out in the crowd.
But each time,
I swear,
you have this grin on your face, as if you enjoy
carrying the weight of everyone's misfortunes.
Grinning like you know you can
save them,
save us,
save me.

Each morning I peer over the balcony to make
sure you have slept well.
I am enamored by all that you are,
but I hope one day you'll have more than this place.
More than a place where things come to be forgotten.

I love you
but please don't end up like me.
Don't stay and watch time fly by minute after minute,
year after year,
I pray for you each night, and ask God,
that you'll get a chance, to move far away,
from here.

To A Sunflower:
A Love Letter from a Picture Frame

I fell in love with you on a Sunday.
The living room was just a blend of your
perfume, coffee, and freshly washed laundry,
I suppose this is what heaven smells like too.

You were staring out the window as you often
do, but, today was different.
You smiled to yourself as your gaze drifted
off into the quiet afternoon, and to this day,
I wonder what you thought about.
I wondered which far away meadow you let
you mind wander off too, whether you could
hear the ocean or blue jays I couldn't quite tell.

You didn't notice, but the rays of sun bounced
around you as if they recognized themselves in
your smile, and you had no clue but, I was
falling in love with you all the while.

I only capture life in moments.
I tend to make memories the root of who I am,
even though you've told me how dangerous
it is to live my life in snapshots.
But you have it all wrong.
I know moments slip through your fingertips no
matter how hard you try to keep them from
running away.
I know one day, your back will hurt and you'll
wilt from the pain of reality, but I live to
capture moments.

So when the golden tint of your youth fades away,
when staring out the window is just a constant
reminder of what could've been, just know, when
you look into my pupils it will always be Sunday
afternoon there.
And you're smiling to yourself as if you and your
dreams have a secret place to escape to.
It's quiet there, because that's the only place
love can truly be, and all the while
I'm watching you, hoping, that whatever world you
run off to, I'm there, keeping you company.

To A Newspaper:
A Love Letter from a Rubber Band

Sometimes I can't stand you.
While it's endearing on most days, the truth
of the matter is it's hard to love a know it all.
And while I enjoy the stories you tell me,
there are some mornings where I wish you'd
just be content to stretch out with me.

To you,
the world has always been black and white
and once something is imprinted onto your
lips, it's hard to convince you otherwise.
But flexibility is my strong suit.
So while we sit on the front porch each
weekend and listen to the crows argue,
I'll show you how sweet the gray area of
this world can be.

My favorite thing about you is the puzzled
look on your face when searching for the
right words to say, and my vocabulary
isn't as extensive, but I enjoy trying to fill
in the blanks for you.
You started off shy but once you opened
yourself up, there were so many things you
wanted to talk about.
You jump so quickly from topic to topic
and I've seen you get disorganized, watched
as your mind seemed to fold over itself until
parts of stories started mixing and matching.

I know the stress of it causes wrinkles around
your cheekbones, and I will be there to hold you.
Whether it be a loose arm around your shoulder,
or a hug so tight it reminds you that even if it
seems that the world is falling apart around you,
I'll always keep you together.

Still

When you are sad,
and you take the batteries
out of your voice box,
I will sit with you
in the stillness.
When you accomplish something,
I will record the moment
between our eyes meeting and
the explosion of our cheers.
I'll record the stillness
and replay it at the highest
volume, when we are old,
I will walk you to the
center of our living room,
I will slow dance with
you to nothing,
In perfect rhythm,
as if we could hear the last
fifty years of our lives,
In the stillness.

To A Sail:
A Love Letter from a Skipping Stone

Your red hair, redder than 1000 cherry-flavored
jawbreakers and a city's worth of fire hydrants
combined, the wind is its dance partner, and
when the sunlight hits just right, It's the perfect show.

That was the first thing I noticed about you.
You made my knees buckle but if you called for me,
I'd go to you in leaps and bounds.
I never understood why they called it relationships,
but perhaps it's because love makes your stomach
turn until you swear you're seasick.
And I'm told that I'm the kind of person who sinks
into where I am that once I go off the deep end it's
hard to find myself again.

But with you. . .
With you I just want to drift along to your sound
waves, and submerge myself in anything that
involves being close to you.
I'm completely enamored by how even though the
crowds chase after you, the only thing you ever pay
attention to is the breeze.
As if the smallest things spoke in orchestras.
That we can sway to while the moon is watching.
And I know I may not be the best person to be with.

This world has jaded me, but that same force
polished my edges, I was made strong.
But this place has also chipped away parts of me,
and I know I can be dense, but I promise I won't
try and anchor you to me.
That's not how love works, and besides, I love you
for that desire to always be free.

Darling,
If it were up to me, I would say you fall in love the
second your heart sinks.
Because once I capsized into your smile, I never
wanted to skip anywhere else again.
So I'd stay there forever.
And that seems like a beautiful life sentence to me.

I would drown in those eyes, and never regret it,
because they're right under the stars.
Just reminders that maybe I'm just a stepping stone
in the grand scheme of things.
The stars, just a chandelier of memories,
I hope to make, with you.

To A Skipping Stone:
A Love Letter from a Sail
By: Heidi Lahl

The first time you flashed that smile
at me I knew I was hooked.
Those eyes of yours pull me in and I admit that
I've tried to drown myself in those blue waters
more than once. That freckled face so loved by
the sun, the way the wind sweeps up your hair
and dances with the edges.

You've made me believe that magic exists in your
fingertips, the way my body turns to goosebumps
every time you play on my back.
I love the way you skip around, never fearful of
falling but just intent on seeing, and on the rare
occasion, when you fall short of where you
thought you'd be, you get right back up and dive
right in.

That must be why everyone searches for you and
do you laugh?
When you see the crowds looking for you along
the shore, each one just wanting to get a glimpse
of you, to hold you for a moment before you run
off again.
I know you think it's silly the way they all obsess
over finding you, but you make everyone's heart
skip a beat when you walk into a room and take
the wind from my lungs every moment,
I spend with you.

I have to admit though, I'm just like the others.
If you gave me a chance, I'd hold you for eternity,
under the stars I'd rock you to sleep, I'd travel the
world till you felt safe in my arms happily,
tethered to your charm for the rest of my days,
let me be the one who gets to live under your sun.

To The Wind:
A Love Letter from the Ocean

If I had to choose my favorite thing about you,
It would be how you've seen everything.
Your stories about camels, Stonehenge,
and how air tastes on Mount Everest, never
fails to make my eyes glaze over.
In truth, I'm a very deep thinker, but somehow,
you manage to tell me things I can never quite
wrap my mind around.

We talk for hours as you glide along to your
next adventure, and as hard as I try, I can't help
but drown in the happiness of it all.
You'll always try to get me to come with you.
When the destination comes into view, you'll
interlock your fingers with mine and race
forward in sheer excitement.
And I know that each time, you're disappointed
when I tell you that running my fingers through
the sand is enough.

The reluctance has nothing to do with you.
And loving you is always a breeze, but, people
don't submerge themselves in me for long, and
I don't dive into what life is like past the sand.
It's just understood, that me and the rest of the
world has a very surface level relationship.
There are parts of me that even I haven't explored yet.
This world is not ready for such unbearable pressure,
not even you.

But sometimes, I want to ask if all that desire to see
what's out there ever leaves you feeling winded.
Honestly, I want to ask if you would stay here with me.
While it's true you've seen many things, have you
ever wondered what you would see if you stayed in
one place, and let it come to you instead?
But I know you hate standing still, so I'm content with
holding your hand as I walk you to your next journey.
Besides, the impact your life has on others is most felt
when you're just passing through.

So when we get to shore,
I'll wave goodbye,
just before you fade out of view.

To A Telescope:
A Love Letter from a Microscope

And there you were.
Gazing out the window as you always do whenever
the moon decides to start its day.
You fixate on all things celestial and I imagine that
your stoic concentration is just a hole ridden quilt
you keep to hide a deep-rooted sadness, of not being
able to grasp what's right in front of you.

I don't want to come off as overly self-confident but,
I know you need me.
The same way the moon needs the sun when he starts
to doze off into morning.
You search for the light at the end of the storm, but
never stop to think that ants see oceans in raindrops.
You crave for land in the middle of the sea, but never
stop and realize that a drop of water can be home.

Does it ever hurt to search through all that
distance alone?
Or is distance just a veil to hide all that fear, that
perhaps things within arm's reach are just not
as beautiful.
That beauty may only exist if some of it is left to
the imagination.
Because up close, planets have jagged edges,
snow isn't spotless, stars fizzle out. . .

And love is messy.
My life revolves around the tiniest of details,
how paint leaves small bubbles when it dries,
how tree trunks twist their spines to reach the sun.
How oil spills are just concrete's way of saying
I can be beautiful too.
Yes, up close it's all messy, but it's also real.

And maybe that's something you need to feel.
Instead of getting lost in the clouds or horizons,
we can get lost in this beautiful mess.
Smiling,
that we have all this noise,
all this imperfection,
all this melancholy,
all this chaos,
to build a masterpiece on.

To A Reflection:
A Love Letter from a Mirror

Above all else, ever since you first looked
at me wide-eyed and curious, as if you saw
parts of yourself hidden in me somewhere,
I want you to know, I have always loved you.

You'd sit there and paint the world superheroes,
princesses, and marshmallow cereal, and from
that moment, I swore I'd do anything for you.

There was a time you refused to smile because
your teeth blossomed crooked, so, I sewed
strings of sunlight to fish out the smile through
your eyes.

I watched you fall in love, and as painful as it
was for me, I always made sure to tell you
what I thought of your outfit, even if you rarely
listened to me.

I watched every milestone,
every holiday
every success
and failure
and everything in between.
And I couldn't help but fall in love more.

But I also watched the world wear you down.
Your face became hard in learning, that the
superheroes don't always win, princesses
don't always live happily ever after and
marshmallow cereal doesn't fix everything.

I watched the tears free fall from your eyes
and for the first time, realized that there are
many forms of shattering.
The other day you genuinely laughed for the
first time in months, but I could tell by your
face that it all sounded like a foreign language
to you.

I wish I could tell you everything I saw, but I'm
not much of a talker, and I was born with a
glass jaw, so, the words weigh too much to say.
But just know I still remember you wide-eyed
and curious.
With the smile I'd sew sunlight to see.
I wish you knew, that I'd always think you're
beautiful, no matter who you turned out to be.
Even if you packed up and moved and we were
oceans apart
Darling, you could lose your leg, and still run
away with my heart.

So, from here, everything about you is
breathtaking from what I can see, and when we
lock eyes, I think you see pieces of yourself
hidden here, and that's more than enough, for me.

To A Magnifying Glass:
A Love Letter from a Violin

There are days when the heat of your gaze
makes me wonder how anything could
survive there.
What will you say?
When you finally focus in on all my flaws?
What will you think, when you see that parts of me
are chipped away or left behind in places you'll
never know about.

Unfinished

Petals

It must be hard being a flower.
People rush to you for assurance,
picking your brain to figure out
if someone loves them or not.

And no matter what
answer you give,
no one ever thinks to thank you
for exhausting yourself over
dilemmas that you don't even own.

It must be hard being a flower,
It must be unfair being a flower,
the world expects you to be
outwardly beautiful just to be
used to explain feelings that people,
can never find the words to.

Bryophyta

To the girl who sat next to me in lecture all
semester, you remind me of moss because
you have this special way of growing on people,
the kind of way that, before I even realized it,
I was already attached to you.

And did you know, God made everyone's
heartstrings out of shoelaces, and maybe
He double knotted ours together because
adventures have unpredictable weather.
And rule number one was always be prepared.

You've got a moss-covered soul and sunlight
in your hair.
You remind me of moss, because you're this
hidden gem of a world.
And perhaps there is global warming in your
voice box, so, whenever you laugh, I always
find myself melting.
And I always stay late to peruse what the
world of yours has been collecting.

So, to the girl that sat next to me in lecture all
semester, we both lead different lives and
we're both pretty busy. . .
But you take the air from my lungs, so, your
smile makes me dizzy.
And you remind me of moss, you're beautiful,
and being with you is easy.

Refill

Isn't it weird?
That if the glass of each friendship
you have with people were filled to
a different level,
If the glass of your best friend was
not overflowing,
or if the glass
didn't fill up to the point where you
could say I love you to that
friend. . .
That was more than a friend.
Or a glass collecting cobwebs was
then filled halfway
If you traded the stories and
memories of one friend,
for that random delivery man
that lives across the hall,
or the glass was filled enough
for them to say I don't hate you after all,
If the cups were refilled,
and you had to sink into all
your friendships again. . .
But at different heights,
how different would you be?

Honeymoon

Dear Sun,

On most nights,
I often get lost in my thoughts of you.
When the rest of the world is sleeping,
I find myself thinking,
how ironic this all is.
That we are only separated by moments where you rise and set,
yet the distance of our relationship is immeasurable.

There are those nights where I want to ask you to move into the same sky.
And I convince myself that the stage is big enough for the two of us.
But the light I blanket this world with pales in comparison to yours.
You have always been that gorgeous.
So, I don't mind loving you from afar.
After all, . . .
I can spend my nights making wishes for you on stars.
I wish that you'd see yourself the way I do.
I wish that you wouldn't feel insecure for being too bright,
I wish you could know,
that your eyes are all I think about each night.

And aside from loving you,
you are someone I've always admired.
Everything seems to grow when you're around.
And I imagine it's because they want to be closer to you too.
I've watched glaciers melt from a single smile,
lions bask in your arms like newborns,
palm trees stretch their leaves out as if they are trying to save
some of you for later,
and even the sky cries when you don't show up to work in the morning.

I must admit that sometimes I get a little jealous.
My hands are not very good at nurturing things,
but I will stay up all night and watch over everything you've created.
I have just enough light to make people fall in love with each other
the same way I fall in love with you.
I can control the tide just enough to scribble love letters onto every
shoreline, so you have something to read when you wake up tomorrow.
I'll tell the constellations stories about a star so warm,
so breathtaking,
so unfathomably beautiful,
that the whole sky is reserved just for her.

And when you wake up and slowly drift into view,
I'll linger behind to get a glimpse of you before I leave,
so that maybe when I sleep, I'll see you in my dreams.
And I know I go through these phases,
where I change my shape and appearance to impress you,
but you've always known the real me so who am I to pretend. . .
We are only separated by moments where you rise and set,
but maybe it's not such a bad thing that the chase for each other will
never end.
I imagine,
that all the chasing will make catching each other that much sweeter.

So,
when the stars align and our worlds eclipse,
I will hold you tightly.
I'll let you peer over my shoulder at all the people who wish they
could hold you in their arms the way I will.
I know you'll be sad that I can only do this twice a year,
but knowing we'll be together again is all I'll ever need,
I could drown in the light of you, Love
and never have to breathe.

Love,
Your Moon

Eclipse

By: Cindy Nguyen

Dear Moon,

It's been a while since I've seen you,
I guess the thrill of the chase had to end sooner or later, right?
You always did say the sky was a little too small for the both of us.

I'm still reminiscing about the last time the stars aligned and our
worlds eclipsed,
finding it hard to find solace in the idea that we never were meant
to live in the same sky.
In truth, it hasn't been the same since you left.
I haven't been the same.

Days are gloomier,
my rays can't extend itself the way they used to,
even the clouds are crying in your absence.

Why didn't you say goodbye?

I'm trying to convince myself that you left with all the right
intentions, with all my best interests.
You always wanted me to take center stage.
So that I can shine a little brighter,
love a little harder,
and finally give my whole self to the world,
instead of always hiding behind the clouds and running
away when life got hard.

You were always the one to save me from the darkness.
I couldn't help but shine my brightest while I was with you.

And I really owe all the best parts of me to you.

Love,
Your Sun

Hammers

Perhaps we are no different
from hammers,
we are made to fix what
is broken.
But secretly,
when the world isn't watching,
we search the stars
and wish that we weren't so good,
at breaking things.

Washing Machine

On those mornings,
when the sun is insecure and peeks
over the clouds' shoulders,
self-conscious because its rays are
simply too beautiful, for days like this one.
Where the backdrop to life is water
colored gray, the kind of morning,
where perhaps even God abuses the snooze button. . .

On these mornings,
my mind likes to watch the reruns of you.
My eyes are fooled by the mirage
of you next to me.
And sometimes,
my shoulders can feel your dreams
as if you are still using them
as pillows.

But these mornings are becoming
increasingly scarce.
Just a resource that I rarely find when I dig through
my life nowadays.
And these mornings last time I checked were
officially on the endangered species list,
and you will ask why I am not doing what I can
to save them, but my climate is just not suitable
for them to survive anymore.
So, we both have just a handful of
these mornings left, just wormholes to travel back
to a time that is untouchable to us now.

Because on most mornings,
I only remember a ghost of you,
but on some days,
you are just as beautiful as I remember.
But the lines are blurring as of late
so, can you blame me for questioning if you
ever existed at all?
On most mornings,
I just cannot help but ask,
did you exist, love?
Because when I think about all the best parts
of my life,
I see your smile out of the corner of my eye.

Did you exist, love?
Because my hands are always searching for
something to hold these days.

Did you exist, love?
Or was I just making promises to a phantom,
how could we build a future?
On promises that break under the pressure.

Did you exist, love?
Because how can something intangible
strangle the heart like this.
How can something disappear into thin air?
But leave the weight of the world for me to carry.

Did you exist, love?
Because when the storms kept rolling in,
I only caught glimpses of you in people
with a better forecast.

Did you exist when I needed you the most?
When I needed you to prove that promises are more than
just paper airplanes swallowed by the sky,
to prove that forever can take a punch to the chin
and not throw in the towel,
to prove that forever does not come delivered in a
box labeled "fragile," to prove that forever is not
just meant for when things are convenient.

On some days,
it is hard to tell if you existed,
because I spoke the best of you,
but no one else seemed to recognize her.
And now I can only remember a ghost of you
because what else is capable of haunting someone
like this?

So, did you exist?
Because on some days I am convinced
I must have dreamt you,
It is true what they say,
lips do not leave imprints,
and fingertips do not trace permanent lines.
So, can you blame me for not remembering
whether or not you were my home?

On most mornings,
I realize my mind is just a washing machine,
and I have run the memories of you
through so many cycles that the colors
are not as vibrant as they used to be.

I have noticed,
that the stars were not dancing off your teeth
like they used to,
and I am convinced I don't have photographic memory,
because when I picture you, the image always comes
out blurry.

And I just have to ask but do you picture
the moment, when we both realized we would not be
everything we promised we would be.
Or when we come up on each other's feed,
does that little piece of your heart that we promised
each other feel like a birthday punch bruise too?
Because on most mornings
It asks me,
"Do you remember her?"
And it is offended every time I respond,
"I barely recognize her now."

Memories

What if memories
are just life's way
of beautifully torturing us.

Midnight on Main Street

On nights like this,
when the city lights look like fireflies ballroom
dancing with lightning bugs.

And women in gold dresses act like shooting
stars in a sea of night sky black tuxedos
granting the wishes of lucky red rose souls.

And the wind is bold enough to make silk
jackets not quite enough and sharing body
heat just right,
I remember the night we first met.

Hi, my name is Xavier.

And I couldn't help but notice the brown
diamonds in your eyes when you glanced
over in my direction, the celestials in
your smile when you caught me staring
a split second too long, the stardust
in your hair from the leftover pieces of
Heaven God used to make you,
and my name in your back dimples
when you walked by me to look out
the window.

Hello, like I said, I'm Xavier.

And you look gorgeous tonight.
And I must say, on nights like this,
as beautiful as the Skyscrapers look in the
moonlight, I feel sorry that they can never
see you up close. The streetlights are just
a way to make sure the spotlight is always
on you. Town cars, just well-dressed taxis
that have traveled all this way to play
an inner-city symphony just for us.

I know right now you're probably thinking
that I'm all talk. That I mask myself
behind meticulously made metaphors and
serenade you with star-related similes.

But I think you should know I've been
undressing you with my eyes for the
last forty-five seconds,
and my hands can work twice as fast,
or slow to accommodate to your liking.

I swear, I'm usually not the kind of guy
to do this, but it is midnight on Main Street.
The city is just a giant nightclub and has been
playing slow songs all night.
And baby when was the last time you really danced?
Even the stars are partnered up for the night.

So, it's common law that no one can be
alone even if it is just for this one moment.
And I can tell you're feeling lonely
because your lipstick hasn't been smeared
by a matching set from a man who meets
the standards of a goddess.

Just for tonight, the cement is the red carpet
and you, you are the star of the show.
Even the moon knows that there's
something more beautiful than it here down
below.

So, if you ask me,
It's the perfect night for seduction.
And the foreplay is just for playing your
body like the only instrument I have
ever seen.
Yes, I've noticed how uncomfortable those
heels are, so take them off and get comfortable.
Your body looks restrained;
let me move those dress straps down
your arms, so nothing holds you back.

You see, I am somewhat of an entertainer so
sit back and enjoy the show.
I will make your mouth whisper my name
like it is your darkest secret,
while your nails carve it into my back, so
you don't forget me when I leave tomorrow.
I will drink all your unspoken intentions of the
night from your neck while I explore your
hourglass body with my fingertips.

I'm sorry, I'm getting a little ahead of myself.
I promise, this isn't a scheme to stand tall
for one night, and I'm willing to wait the
designated amount of time it takes to cook
a perfect dish of intimacy even if it
takes years or more. Because before we
even met I was fairly sure my heart
was already yours.

Just give me a moment of your time to
persuade you. The night is still young,
and we are just getting older.
I know you feel that the nighttime breeze
is getting colder.
Can I wrap my arms around your shoulders?
Don't leave yet, please, the waiter came by,
and I said table for two, I already told him.

If you let me,
I'll turn this moment when the
sun is oblivious to our nighttime vendettas
while it is sleeping, into everything two
strangers could possibly want.

If you let me,
I'll show you my reasons for acting overly
zealous.
Me and you something beautiful at
midnight to make the skyline jealous.

If you let me,
I'll warm every inch of you,
every skin cell,
and every bone.

If you let me,
I promise,
this will be the last midnight
you'll ever spend alone.

Before We Know It

To you,
I just wanted to say that I hope the drive to
work today wasn't so stressful, and that
the coffee you always order, from that
hipster cafe on the corner,
was made just right,
and before I forget,
I hope you slept well last night.
I hope you took that walk along the beach,
and that the ocean waves didn't seem too rough,
I know you're always busy,
but I hope you're remembering to eat enough.
I hope you're watching the sunset and know
that it gets jealous watching you,
and if you've been feeling a little lonely,
just know somewhere in the world,
I'm stuck thinking about you.

I know this makes absolutely no sense to
send you paper airplane-shaped wishes
about the smallest parts of your day.
Especially, when the turbulence of everyday
life seems to crinkle its wings, so they never
seem to land on your mind. And it isn't your
fault at all, because words and wishes can
sometimes lose strength when traveling
from one heart to another, you know it's
weird I'm telling you this, because we
don't even know that we're supposed
to be in love with each other.

So, if we fall in love tomorrow,
I hope we have
that "steal all my sweaters" type love,
that "summer night breeze weather" type love,
that "when we're together,
the world seems better" type love,
that "every other girl is just whatever" type love,
I hope we have that
"I love you even though you're a mess" type love,
that "you don't even have to guess" type love,
that "you can have my best" type love,
that "the world can have the rest" type love.

To Death

Dear Death,
Growing up I didn't know you,
But can you blame me?
After all, doesn't God first tell the
butterfly to live, to stretch its wings
and take in as much of Life as possible?
So how am I any different from that?
They told me to live.
And so, I did.
Can you blame me?

I never knew you, but I saw you take things.
You took away strangers to remind me of
your existence.
You took away the elderly to remind me that
no story lasts forever.
You took away the young to remind me that
like Life, you aren't fair.
You took away loved ones to remind me that
you were close by.
You took away the rich and powerful to
remind me that status is not salvation.
You took away life to remind me that in the
end, we are all equal.
You came for many but left with few to
remind me, that in some cases, you
were merciful.

Growing up I was scared of you.
But can you blame me?
They told me to live.
To reap the rewards of anything my will so
happened to touch,
to squeeze every drop of joy I could
get out of the fruits of life.
But they never mentioned you.
So, I came to fear you.
Because you were a constant reminder of
my own mortality.
Can you blame me, Death?
For what is a greater fear than something
that is both known and unknown all at
once?

Now I am learning to understand you.
And this yin-yang trapeze act you play
with Life, and how fragile the balance
really is.
And maybe they were wrong to tell us
all to live.
They should have said right from our
first breath,
one day you will die,
so, live as fully and as deeply as you can,
while you still can.

So, Dear Death,
I am learning about you now so when
I am old,
when my hair is the color of
tombstones and skies that make you
forget what sunlight is like,
when I have accomplished everything,
I set out to do,
when you arrive,
you won't be a stranger,
and we can walk side-by-side,
As friends.

A Letter from Flight 13

Dear you,
I want this to be as clear as possible:
Thank you.
Thank you for being a wishing well wish come true.

You.
Just a three-letter reason to why the world has seemed
a little more beautiful than usual lately.

You.
The three letters in the alphabet I loved more than "I".

You.
The first thing that comes to mind whenever I think of:
saltwater taffy, and sandcastles, and getting in trouble,
and make sure to step in every puddle, a rose that grows
from piles of rubble, how everything was a game, and
midnight kisses drenched in rain, and I'm attracted to
how you're strange, what I'd choose over the money,
the glory, and the fame.

A synonym for delight, Saturday mornings flying kites,
reminding me don't let the bedbugs bite,
a copilot who I hoped would like to take this flight.

You.
The reason why half of the bed has been vacant for
three months, five days, sixteen hours, twenty minutes,
and thirty seconds.

You.
The pronoun that reminds me that I'm just a
modern-day Atlas destined to carry the weight of the
world on my shoulders alone.

You.
The one thing God stole from me along with my smile.

You.
A one-word sentence that states why I even bother
getting up in the morning even though a part of me
is lifeless.

You.
The only thing I love and hate because you made
me care about you and let me tell you it sucks to
genuinely care about somebody.

You.
The only person I wish I could still give the world
too like before.
Please come back.
I really miss you.
Love,
A lonely copilot waiting for takeoff.

Raindrops

And maybe,
raindrops are just tears
the clouds shed when they are
too far away from you.
Frustrated, that all they can do
is drift along with you but
never reach out to grab your
hand along the way.
Maybe that's why they free fall
from the heavens,
without a second thought,
trusting nothing,
but the notion,
that Heaven can't
be anyplace without you.

The Crossroad

We've walked together on the same road for my entire life.
You, me, and this road we have been laying the foundation to.
I'll be the first to say that the time spent overcoming the
roadblocks and enjoying the times where the road seemed to
be smoother than marble, are moments that I will always
remember. But like all roads, we will eventually come to a
crossroad, and because life does not always allow for
ideal situations, I will go one way. You will have to go the
other. Please do not be too alarmed because our individual
roads will cross countless more times in the future.
However, understand that for this new journey,
we must be apart.
So, before we are both too busy setting foundations for
our new roads, let me tell you things that I love.
Then maybe, when you wish I was here, you'll find
some comfort until next time.

I love the cold side of pillows. I know it seems like something
very minute, but the idea of having something refreshing
to welcome you after a hard day's work is very important.
*So, when you are tired after traveling without me, make sure
you have a cold pillow; you'll thank me later.*

I love early mornings. Being the only one awake lets you appreciate the simple things in nature. From the smell of crisp air to the peaceful silence, early morning is the closest anything gets to being perfect. Maybe my love for it comes from when you used to take me to get pork buns right when the bakeries, two blocks down, opened at sunrise.

You would tell me stories about how things were before I was born. You'd tell me about growing up in the Philippines, my Grandpa Eddie, and occasionally about something funny you saw on TV the night before.

Stories turned into lessons and those lessons turned into telling me about your hopes and dreams for me as I made my own way in the world. Back then I was only four years old and too young to understand the concept of growing up. But maybe you told me early in my life so that one day, I could come to understand the reasons behind why you made the decisions you had to make so that I could pursue my own dreams.

So, while we are traveling apart, remember to catch a sunrise or two, because I'll be watching them too.

I love the feeling of right when an airplane takes off.
Every time we went on a family trip, you'd stay up the whole
night before. You told me that it was because you had to pack
the clothes, the toothbrushes, the contact solution,
all the phone chargers, numerous shampoos, and the camera,
but I knew it was because you were the most excited out of
the four of us. When that moment came on the runway, after
the hectic process of checking in, going through security,
and of course waiting, no one had a bigger smile on their
face than you. With the anticipation of a new adventure,
whether it be Hawaii or London, I could not blame you for
having that goofy grin on your face, even half an hour after
takeoff. One time in particular, during my brother and I first
time on an airplane, I'm pretty sure you went through about
five disposable cameras before we even landed at our
destination, which was only an hour away from San Francisco.
I know I complained about all the photos but thank you for
preserving special moments like that. You have made finding
a throwback Thursday photo for Instagram that much easier.
*So, when the normalcy of walking down the usual road starts
to make you wish we could all be on a plane again to some
mysterious place, remember that waiting will make that
feeling of takeoff that much sweeter.*

I love mangoes. I would not be satisfied until I ate about five on my own, and even though you knew I'd get sick from eating so many, you never hesitated to peel the yellow skin and cut them for me. To be honest, when I was a kid, I used to think you were some kind of magician when it came to picking mangoes, or any fruit for that matter. I remember how proud I was when I went to a store all by myself to buy you a box that turned out to be some of the worst mangoes I'd ever eaten. Then the next day you bought some from the same store and they tasted like they were from God's own garden. You always had that magic touch. From cooking to taking care of all of us when we got sick, you performed wonders with those hands I cannot fully explain to this day. But the most memorable time would have to be the mangoes. Needless to say, I let you pick all the fruits from that point forward.

So, when you come across a roadblock during your journey, just remember that you have always been able to find a solution to the most impossible of situations.

I love the sound of rain. When the rainfall was at just the right
speed and at just the right amount, I wouldn't have any
problem falling asleep. I also knew that when the rainfall was
just right, you'd take me to the window, and we'd race the
rain drops down to the bottom. We'd sit there for about five
minutes waiting until there were enough droplets that we
could race. I know it seemed like I was impatient,
but those five minutes listening to the rain was like hearing
the Earth speak. Of course, I never took my mind off the
race, and I, being the most competitive person you've ever
known, would let you choose one first so I could find a drop
that was already half a length ahead of yours. I know you
noticed when halfway through the race, I'd change my
raindrop because I was losing. So, thank you for allowing
me to gain confidence through victory, it helped me down
the road to find confidence in defeat.
So, when it starts to rain on your parade,
and you just so happen to feel like the losing droplet,
remember that there's another race to be won right around
the corner.

I love your support. No matter what it was, you were always there. At every basketball game I played in, you were in the stands. It never mattered if we won by twenty or lost by twenty; after the game, I still seemed like a champion to you. Your unwavering support taught me that effort is more important than outcomes. You were there for all my spoken word performances, and after I managed to get through a three-minute poem on stage you always cheered a little bit louder and clapped a bit longer than everyone else, yes, I noticed. When I was five and decided that being a dinosaur was what I was going to do with my life, you watched Jurassic Park 1, 2, and 3 with me numerous times to make sure my T-rex roar was perfect. When I decided to leave home to go to college, to be on my own knowing that I would have to deal with a lot of life's problems by myself, you told me I could come back anytime.

So, to repay you for all the things you have done, know that while you adjust to life with me being a little less present, I'll be supporting you.

Take care of yourself while I'm gone, and of course, Xander and Dad as well.
We'll be on the same path together soon.
I love you.

Fireflies

I don't remember how old I was when I decided
that there were fireflies in your veins.
Millions of nature's light bulbs moving warp
speed across your anatomy.
And every so often, when one just so happens
to find its way to your retinas, the light projects
out of your pupils and I get a glimpse of 1984
and the 18-year-old version of you.
I see a young, brash adolescent sporting jean
shorts because that was in back then.
And of course, a muscle tee because
The Terminator changed your life.
The perfect mix of being confident enough
to love but not cocky enough to hate.

You have the same look in your eyes that
you do now.
Only sharper and more determined.
I can see why mom always says I look
just like you, a flat top haircut that seemed
to defy gravity the way it stood on your head,
while you leaned back on your gray Nissan.
As if mocking Father Time letting him know
you will be young forever.

And I wonder, where does this boy go when
the business world decides that youth is just a
distraction from a Dream that America makes
seem so attainable?

Where does he run off to when society implies
that children don't belong in the usual
nine to five?

I still see flashes of him every so often even if
it's for just split seconds at a time.
I hear him in your jokes when the first seasons of
The Cosby Show and *The Fresh Prince of Bel-air*
seem to go hand in hand while you drop the
punchline.

You're the best reverse driver I've ever met.
And maybe the young you is just a more stocky,
Filipino version of Marty McFly coming back to
the future to tell you to not grow up so fast.

Thanksgiving Day 2005, I saw the way your eyes
lit up when you heard the *Ghostbusters'* theme
song as if you had just come in contact with a
friend from years ago.
And lately, you've been playing this app on your
iPad where you build your own Utopia, and I bet
that it's just your subconscious teenage
self-trying to tell you that you can still make
This world the way you want it.
Generations of younger you trapped on the
wrong side of your hourglass shouting at the top
of their lungs that youthful creativity is what has
made mankind such beautiful beings.
I've seen you come home from the store with a
Bluetooth stereo we didn't even need, but maybe
that's just him trying to tell you that childlike
spontaneity makes life that much more meaningful.

Whenever you give me that awkward man hug
you do, I smell Mission Street in the summer with
its excellent Taquerias and the up-beat lifestyle of
having no worries.

And when I look at you now, I can still see
Fillmore Street back in the eighties hiding in the
gray hairs, that street you lived on where people
were able to label you minority, but youth gave
you enough naivety to escape from what the real
world was like.
What would it be like if that little boy could see
Fillmore now and what it has become?
The small family shops metamorphosing into
five-star restaurants and the rough neighborhood
becomes a city hot spot for tuxedo and cocktail
dress dates.
Would he be proud of the change?
Or say that the place he called home sold out to
make way for the finer things in life?

Let me meet this boy once to see if he really was
just like me.
I know we both wanted to be Michael whether
Jordan or Jackson it never mattered.
Just as long as we were on top of the world.
We wanted to be kings.
Only the firefly light that sparked your passions
has decided to ride back seat to everything else.

Did you fight like I did?
Fight the idea of letting growing up take away
the child in you?
Don't be ashamed to say no, because I notice
every time I leave the house to go somewhere,
a part of you jerks toward me.
Sometimes I think it's that boy with the gravity
defying high top trying to break free of the black
hole of your Hippocampus and be more than just a
"what I used to be."

So please,
keep wearing those shirts with the soda
brands on them,
keep buying the shoes that are in style,
keep trying to use Facebook,
keep using the word "hashtag" at the most
random, inappropriate times,
and somewhere in that nine-to-five grind,
remember that there's a part of you that's
still eighteen, and that part can live
harmoniously with the
Mr. Miyagi outlook you have on life.
Trust me,
It keeps the fireflies going.

Thank you

Featured on YouTube @stmarys-ca.edu December 3, 2015.
"Gratitude can be expressed in countless ways. Psychology major, Xavier
Echon, chooses spoken word to say thank you to all those who make a
Saint Mary's education possible."

Thank you for being modern day Atlases,
Supporting jigsaw pieces of our worlds and
our futures on your shoulders.

Thank you.
For holding onto nothing more than faith and understanding
that we can't do it all alone and becoming guardian angels
to young adults you've never even met.

Thank you.
For those moments made possible by you.
Those moments where 2:00 a.m. 's look over the shoulders
of students who understand that sometimes to earn that A,
to pass that class, to shake hands with success requires the sacrifice
of sleep.

That is all thanks to you.
That instant where it all comes down to the last shot,
the last goal, the last sprint, the last strand of willpower,
in the name of victory.

That is all thanks to you.
Where "I think I can."
Turns into "I know I can."
Where anxiety filled eyes turn into
Powerful voices,
Kicking down the door of opportunity,
Yelling in full confidence,
"I am here!
And I am going to change this world for the better if it's the
last thing I do with my time here on Earth."
That is all thanks to you.

Thank you.
For being the gardeners who nurtured the seeds of all our dreams.
In the simplest description:
The belief of one human being is the catalyst for success in another
from the bottom of my heart
and the hearts of students like me
whose journey toward greatness
was supported by you,
Thank you.
For the belief.

FXCK CANCER

Illustrated and Designed by Josh Lau
In Collaboration with Adapt Clothing

When Evan gave me the opportunity to help design a shirt about my journey these past two years, I had a difficult time deciding what I wanted this shirt to represent. In two years, I've dealt with cancer, a limb amputation, chemo, and then this relentless grind in order to now have a normal life as a student. What design could possibly capture such extreme feelings of loss and triumph?

As I thought about it, I kept thinking about the question that, to this day, I get asked most frequently: "How do you do it?"

Truth is, my answer to that question has always been ambiguous because

I've never really understood how I did it either.

One day it clicked, and I realized this "secret" has two fundamental parts, and what better way to share that with you than through the design of my shirt.

The first part of the secret is represented by the "X." At a basic level, "X" is a symbol that represents me the most, after all, it's been the nickname I've identified with my whole life. On a deeper level, "X" is a variable that can have an infinite number of values. Despite everything that's happened to me, there are no limitations on what I can do in life. In no way does cancer and my amputation limit my ability to be great. The process may be more challenging, and it may take a more unconventional route, but it's nothing compared to my desire to know what my potential is. The first part is believing that, no matter what obstacles you face in life, only you have the ability to put value to your "X" as long as you embrace the process of solving for it.

The second part of my secret is all of you.
I could have all the willpower in the world, and it wouldn't come close to the amount of strength I continue to receive from my family, my friends, and even people I've never met.
No one is self-made, and I won't lie and say I did this on my own.
In fact, even the design of the shirt is a collaboration of ideas between Evan, myself, and my best friend Josh Lau.

There's a phrase on the back of the shirt that says,
"I really do this."
On the surface level, it's a statement I use when I accomplish another goal on my "comeback story."
But on a deeper level it's just part of the statement.
"I really do this for you."
You're giving me the opportunity to pay it forward and help others by donating all the proceeds to the American Cancer Society and UCSF Benioff Children's Hospital Oakland Oncology Patients.

Whether you were part of my journey from the beginning or just for a part of it,
thank you for believing in me and I love you all.

X

VI

The Eulogy

Xavier Edward James Celestino Echon was born in San Francisco, California, in 1994, and lived there with his mom, dad, and younger brother for twenty-four years. Growing up in the Sunset District, he experienced a relatively quiet upbringing. I remember him saying that what he loved most about living there was, on a particularly amazing day, he could look out towards the ocean, smell the salt water in the breeze, and imagine all life had to offer him if he worked hard enough.

If you ever passed by Xavier on the street, you would immediately think to yourself that this guy is cold or unfriendly. He was one of the kindest and funniest people if you took the time to get to know him. X always cared deeply about the close friends he made in his lifetime, and trust me, there were many. He'd never admit it, but he had a sensitive side, and it especially showed when he was with his loved ones.

Xavier was the first in his family to attend a four-year college and, after graduating from Sacred Heart Cathedral Preparatory high school, enrolled at Saint Mary's College of California. It's funny, he worked so hard all the time but was never satisfied with anything he did, even if it was almost perfect. But I secretly believe that he enjoyed the idea of always continuing to be better. Although more on the introvert side, he immersed himself in anything that interested him including APASA, Asian Cultural Night, Intramural basketball, almost daily visits to the Rec Center, and the sheer bliss of just being a college student. Reflecting on his brief but amazing life, I find myself thinking about all the wonderful things I will miss about Xavier. I will miss the loyalty he showed to all he cared about. Even when you messed up or even if life was not going your way, he would always be there for you. He really knew how to make people laugh, he was witty, and almost always had something funny to say.

I'll miss how motivated he was to be successful, even if sometimes he neglected his health or loved ones to do so. I got to talk to Xavier about it, and he said, "I have to be successful, in fact I'm obsessed with the idea of it. I'm blessed to have so many people that love and believe me, and I believe I owe it to them to be as great as I can be." He put his heart into everything whether it was schoolwork, his relationships, a cheesy spoken word about love, every weight he lifted at the gym, or every second he was on the basketball court, you always knew he'd give his all.

But most of all, I will miss how he was always there when you needed him. Xavier wasn't the type to be the focus of attention, but everyone knew that if you really needed to sit down and talk about something, he was your guy. He always knew what needed to be said, and more importantly, he knew how to listen. It's hard to find that nowadays, a person who will genuinely listen to you and make you feel unafraid of opening yourself up. He was one of them.

I'll truly miss Xavier and getting to watch an amazing story unfold before my eyes. I hope he watches over all of us and that he gives us all a piece of that humble, yet amazing strength to chase our dreams and live life to the absolute fullest.

Being Forever Resilient

Featured in the *Nob Hill Gazette's*, "Perspective on Beauty", March 2019 issue.

As a native San Franciscan, I've had the privilege of growing up in a place where beauty is never in short supply. A place that is often blanketed in fog hides within it a rich blend of history and culture. One minute you're staring wide-eyed at the wall-sized murals of the Mission, or getting lost in the narrow streets of China Town, and the next minute you could be at the very top of Turtle Hill or find yourself in a place where 19,596 people chant "Waarrriiioorrs" in unison.

It's more than reasonable to say that these places capture the essence of the beauty the Bay Area has to offer; however, the real beauty is found in the diverse story of each individual that calls this place home.

When I was twenty-one, I was diagnosed with bone cancer. The word 'shocked' was an understatement, I was young, active, healthy, and I just couldn't comprehend how this was the hand I was dealt because the diagnosis contradicted how I lived my life. One second, I'm a junior in college and the next I'm in chemo for eight months. I'm away from my friends, I have to amputate my right leg, and I get rediagnosed over and over again. The twenty-one-year-old Xavier would have a hard time explaining what beauty meant to him because the world around him seemed dark and ugly. However, at twenty-four, I have gained more of a mature perspective of what beauty really means.

Beauty is resilient.
Beauty is never giving up even if you receive heart breaking news over and over again. It's shattering but choosing to pick up the pieces and remaking yourself into something better.
Beauty is walking the stage at graduation and more so seeing your mom's face as you receive a diploma. Beauty is the person you love most on this earth refusing to leave even if the waters of life get rough. Beauty is not

running from the storm but laughing while thunderclouds of doubt and fear try to drench your spirits.

Beauty is not fragile.

Beauty is the product of every second of struggle.

It's realizing that not everything can be beautiful and things that are beautiful come from the most difficult moments.

Butterflies have to break out of their own cocoons for people to see their wings and coal must do well under pressure to become a diamond.

In the past few years, my life has gone through the most extreme circumstances, and while I'm not totally cured, I still feel this fire inside me that wants, even needs, to keep pushing myself each day. I believe the best is yet to come for me and all the dreams I have are still well within my grasp. Sure, people can throw out all sorts of statistics and facts, but I'm more than a number and no matter how much time I have left I'm going to make the most of it.

And perhaps that's what beauty truly is.

Days after submitting this essay to the Nob Hill Gazette, Xavier Echon died peacefully on January 13, 2019, at home with his family. He was 24 years old.

TESTIMONIALS

For those who have become jaded and calcified by the misfortunes of the human experience, vulnerability is often perceived as weakness. We have a propensity to modify and suppress our emotions in fear of the unknown, and would rather forge our identities into something unrecognizable than tell the truth about ourselves. But Xavier Echon understood that vulnerability is our most valuable asset—it allows us to unlock the uncharted terrain of our hearts and achieve our true potential as human beings. Fortunately, through his art, X exemplifies how one can relinquish emotional boundaries to discover the most remarkable version of ourselves. His wisdom was beyond his years—a result of living through the joys and perils of a thousand lifetimes—and he was generous enough to share what he had learned along the way. In this collection of work, he redefines masculinity, challenges our conceptions of love, and illuminates the darkness to reveal what beauty lies in the unseen.

This book is more than just an extraordinary anthology. X reminds you who he was, and who he knew we could all become. You remember that when you met him, you became engulfed by his moonlight aura and consumed by his sunbeam glow. When we become paralyzed amidst the petrifying chaos of life's uncertainties, X—even in his memory—is there to remind us that our lives are merely a collection of metaphors waiting to become poetry. The legato of his voice always provided a flowing rhythm for our dancing souls, while his words helped us uncover emotions that we never knew existed. Even the darkest forces within us knew to welcome the light he so graciously shared, an enigma that left our inner demons yearning to become angels. This revelation came as no surprise when you witnessed his ability to wire-walk on the tightrope of life's extremes, effortlessly balancing between the spectrum of survival and death, fear and bravery, love and hate.

There is no better example of his brilliant mind than his profound introspections regarding relationships. X was never afraid to expose the depths of his soul for the sake of love despite experiencing the most painful consequences of such an endeavor. X refused to adopt a fatalistic perspective of the world. It takes a valiant being to reject the resentment and antipathy that accompanies heartbreak, and to instead choose to transform it into a source of unmitigated hope for what may still lie ahead. He converted his trials and tribulations into smiles and celebrations. He knew tomorrow was never promised, yet he always made promises for tomorrow. He found a way to fall in love with the darkness of midnight, for he knew it signaled the possibilities of a new day.

His chosen purpose in life was to love so deeply that those who were lucky enough to receive it would feel his presence in every waking moment. To that end, he fulfilled his duty on this earth. What an honor it is to hear his voice in these pages. What a blessing it is to know he is still here.

-Sy Stokes

The FXCK Cancer shirt was a project that hit particularly close to home for me, as I was currently going through my own cancer journey. A friend and employee of mine Hepsie shared with me in mid 2017 that her cousin Xavier was currently going through treatments, and wanted to connect us to possibly work on a fundraising tee together through the charitable Adap+ arm of Adapt.

Upon messaging with and then meeting X, I connected with his story and really felt strongly about working on a tee with him. He was smart, young, full of ideas, and excited about life, which resonated with me all the more as I felt that even at my age I was too young to be battling something like this. But he was just getting started in life, and I could see that he had already endured so much.

The FXCK Cancer tee was a bold statement that we felt incorporated the frustrations of the disease, as well as a statement that it would not hold X back in his life. We used the 'X' logo designed by his friend Josh in place of the 'U' as a way to incorporate his name while also making the graphic a bit more family friendly. The back text reads 'I really do this', as when he would be asked if he was going to beat cancer, he responded with, 'Yes, because I really do this'.

Rest in Peace X.

-Evan

For the last few years, X has been one of my biggest inspirations in life in anything that I've done. Although we only had a few conversations, they were always meaningful and I always learned something from them. I'd say there are three main lessons that I learned through being around X.

Lesson number one: always be grateful for life's blessings. More often than not, we tend to take the simple things in life for granted. The people around us, the ability to walk, the food on the table, the breath of fresh air. Whenever I spoke to X, we always told each other how much we inspired each other and always made sure to show appreciation. In talking to him, although the cards were stacked against him, he never complained and was always grateful to even be playing the game and rising to the challenge.

Lesson number two: control what you can, be at peace with what you can't. X told me that one of the biggest things he learned while being in the hospital came from his nurse practitioner and friend named Megan. She told him to control the 10 percent of things that were in his hands, which included his effort in doing the right things that he needed to do for his recovery. The rest of it, the remaining 90 percent, was out of his hands and he just needed to trust that he was doing everything he could in the 10 percent that he could control and that was more than enough. The way that X worked so hard and was able to be at peace with knowing that he was doing his part of the job was inspiring for me to see and serves as an example for the way that I strive to live my life now. As long as we do our part and truly do our best, that's all that we can really ever ask ourselves for.

Lesson number three: keep striking. At the end of our interview, I asked X for one message he'd like to leave people with. So, he told the story: "there was a stone cutter, who shapes stones by hitting a rock. He'll hit it 100 times and nothing will happen. But then the very next time he hits it on the 101 try, it splits the rock. It's not the one strike that did it, but it's all the strikes put together that broke the rock. Even though it looks like the work isn't adding up right away, eventually, it accumulates together, and you accomplish big things."

X, thank you for being you. You continue to inspire me every single day. I love you brother. See you again one day.

-Jordan Jimenez

I first met Xavier when he came into my cognitive science course in the fall semester of 2015. Of all the courses I teach, this is my toughest, and in my opinion (and students would agree), the most difficult of all courses in the psychology department because of the theoretical, abstract nature of studying the mind. What immediately struck me about Xavier was not his intelligence (which he has plenty to spare) — no... what clearly popped out was that while his passion and love of learning was second to none, his enthusiasm, *his enthusiasm* for learning left everyone in the dust. Xavier›s eagerness, his energy, his vibrance were animated in his actions and words, exuded from his pores, and shone in his eyes. And it was contagious. I taught two sections of cognitive science that fall, the first section had twenty-three students and the second section (Xavier›s) had twenty-one students. By midterm, there were only seventeen students left in section 1 (losing 5-6 students is normal for my cognitive science courses) but Xavier›s cohort only lost two students. Only two students dropped from Xavier›s section. And I KNOW it was because of Xavier›s presence in the class. He embraced the class and its many assignments and difficult exams, and his energy and enthusiasm sustained his classmates. Xavier and Charles Molina (one of his closest friends) put together an outstanding Prezi presentation for a semester project, so excellent that I continue to use it as an exemplar for my cognitive science courses. Years later, Xavier would continue to puzzle on how he didn›t understand why students didn›t/don›t love cognitive science. He was quite confused. LOL. Xavier carried that passion, that love, that enthusiasm, of and for learning, into my experimental research course in the spring semester of 2018. I did not know, could not fathom, there was another level to Xavier›s vivacity. Oh, how wrong I was! By then, Xavier had been battered and exhausted physically, mentally, and emotionally from the ravages of cancer, surgeries, chemotherapy, and physical therapy; and yet he burst into my course, with his new leg, with the same indefatigable and relentless energy and fervor, full of enthusiasm to learn!! And Xavier's intelligence?? OH MY. For my combined cognitive science sections, there were only three A's earned out of forty-four students, and Xavier was the top A. And the 1 1/2 years battling cancer did nothing to stop Xavier from earning the only

A in his cohort of twenty students in my experimental course! *There are NO adjectives.*

I am bawling. I am bawling as I reflect and memory-walk in my mind, recollecting all the wonderful, treasured memories I have of my interactions and chats with Xavier over the three years I know him. As much as Xavier was exceptional in the classroom and an exceptional student, he was an even better person. Xavier is a gift from God. To know Xavier is to experience a phenomenon, to experience a **FORCE** of nature. Towards the end of the spring of 2016, right before summer, Xavier came into my office to tell me that he had been diagnosed with aggressive cancer in his knee and that most likely he would need an amputation, and that he would be taking a leave of absence. I was shocked like I was just hit by a truck (I just had him in class! I›ve been chatting with him in the hallways regularly that semester!), but even as I was trying to process the news, I remember vividly his uplifting spirit, energy, and outlook. Yes, Xavier was scared, revealed by the slightest tremble in his voice, but he was pure positivism! I›ve never known a more positive, courageous person. He assured me that he was going to be fine. Xavier took a leave of absence, but we started conversing through email, with Xavier keeping me updated on his progress. That same fall semester, my daughter started having seizures and it was due to a brain tumor that had emerged in her left brain. The surrealness of it was something that Xavier was going through, so I revealed my daughter›s condition to him. And even as Xavier was suffering from his aggressive cancer and chemotherapy, and at this time, the reality that his leg needed to be amputated, Xavier sent many emails consoling me!! He would encourage me with positive messages like "I'm sending you, your daughter, and your whole family my positive vibes, prayers, and love." What a truly amazing person, worrying about my daughter Jade in the midst of his own long, draining fight with cancer! That is Xavier.

Xavier went on to get his amputation and continued his chemotherapy and while Jade continued her seizures and we continued to stay in touch. Even when his cancer came back with aggression late in 2016, Xavier continued to inspire me (who is the adult here??) with his energy, positive presence, and undefeatable aura, and through his amazing actions. He created, posted, and shared his inspiring videos. Xavier's words and videos gave me strength and hope for Jade. **WHO IS THIS YOUNG MAN??!** In the summer of 2017, Xavier came into my office to deliver the good news that the cancer was in remission, and he would be coming back to classes. I was thrilled for him. But what was to be me listening and supporting and congratulating Xavier, he turned our conversation around to my daughter and we spent the next 90 minutes with him listening and encouraging me to stay strong! That is Xavier. **WHO IS THIS YOUNG MAN??!**

I was devastated when Louie Legacion, another one of Xavier's closest friends, suddenly emailed me on January 13 that Xavier had passed away. Xavier had decided not to disclose that the cancer had returned with a vengeance, with devastation. The shock of Xavier announcing his cancer to me was nothing remotely close to Louie's disclosure of Xavier's passing. I was hit with a profound sense of loss, of sadness, emptiness, and surrealness. NOTHING, I am certain, compared to how Rosalie, Ron, Xander, and the rest of their family must have felt. The world became incredibly dimmer on January 13, 2019. In the early months, when I thought of Xavier, my mind melted and my heart cried, for him, for his life cut short. But now, my heart and mind burst with emotions — all wonderful ones with a touch of wistfulness/of sadness, but only because I miss him.

Xavier, you are simply and absolutely AMAZING; you inspire me like NO ONE ever has. I am in awe of your energy, your strength, your positivity, your optimism. Your light is a beacon of courage, inspiration, and magnificence that shines and bathes us all in goodness. Through your writings, your reflections, your videos, *through your eyes,* I witnessed **HOPE and LIFE** and I realized my own life has been blessed, and graced, and humbled, for knowing you. Keep swishing those jump shots into that heavenly hoop X!

-Hoang Vu

I first met Xavier Echon in a corner hospital room on the sixth floor of UCSF Children's Hospital Oakland. As a pediatric oncology nurse practitioner, I've entered many hospital rooms to meet a young patient on what is usually considered the worst day of their life. Meeting X was quite different. He burst onto the oncology unit and into my life like a dash of love and pure light. At twenty-one years old, he seemed to have already figured out the meaning of life and was patiently waiting for the rest of us to get on board.

With a sense of responsibility and determination, X took on his cancer diagnosis and treatment. He was always looking to recover faster, stronger. He took his task seriously, reducing his college workload and avoiding social interactions that may risk infections. Despite all of these limitations, X never stopped living. The hospital became his classroom, his bedside hand weights became his gym. He befriended every nurse and resident, cracking jokes and engaging in deep, philosophical conversations.

During this time, I noticed X's words grew more and more central to his identity. Cancer had confined him to a hospital room - so he turned to language to engage with the world. X was not only able to find his own power through writing, but he generously gives voice to the intricate feelings of others. His gift for empathy and his love of life are beautifully reflected in his art. For the few short years I spent as X's nurse and friend, I feel incredibly grateful. For those who didn't know him, it is my great privilege to introduce him to you now through this collection.

-Meghan Eaton

We would like to express our love and gratitude to the following:

To Saint Mary's College of California (SMC), thank you for all the memorable experiences, and for the support, which made difficult times bearable. We would like to thank the Psychology Department, where Xavier was challenged and inspired academically, and was recognized with the Frederick Whelan Award. To the Rec Center, thank you for being a place where Xavier could challenge himself physically and competitively. To APASA, thank you for being a space where he could form lifelong friends, and for giving him the opportunity to perform his spoken word poems. We are especially grateful for Luminaria, for having allowed Xavier to speak at the 2018 Relay for Life. To this day, we continue to find comfort and healing watching the video you took of him speaking. And to the *Class of 2017* and *Class of 2018*, thank you for all the friendships and memories you made with Xavier. Thank you for making so many ordinary moments, extraordinary.

To the medical staff, nurses, and ancillary personnel from the Oncology, Surgery, Radiation Oncology, Radiology, Laboratory, and Pathology departments at UCSF Benioff Children's Hospital Oakland, Mission Bay, and Parnassus Campuses – thank you all. Your unwavering support and patience were instrumental in helping Xavier and our family through chemotherapy, multiple surgeries, imaging appointments, and various treatments.

To the Christian Brothers of SHC and SMC, thank you for your constant support and unrelenting prayers for Xavier and our family. God bless everyone.

To Sacred Heart Cathedral Preparatory (SHC), "Enter to Learn, Leave to Serve". Thank you for the poetry slam, basketball games, dances, and other events which helped shape his character; we are so grateful. And to the *Class of 2013*, thank you for all the friendships and memories you made with Xavier.

To Saint Cecilia School and Parish, "The Finest, The Greatest, and The Best". Thank you for the strong academic and spiritual foundation instilled through the faculty, staff, and Sister Marilyn, which gave Xavier the confidence to tackle any challenges he faced. To his coaches, teammates, friends, and the *Class of 2009*, thank you for all of the stories and memories that we will cherish forever.

To Monsignor Michael Harriman, thank you for the spiritual counsel to Xavier and us all, and for teaching him of God's word and miracles. Thank you for always keeping him in your prayers, and for any time you took to visit or reach out to him. Your thoughtfulness was very appreciated. Thank you as well for helping set up the mass for Xavier's viewing, we feel immensely blessed by your support. *God is Good.*

To the BAAS Dragons organization, Xavier's teammates, their parents, and coaches of the Red Dragons *Class of 2013* – thank you for the opportunity that allowed Xavier to be a part of the team. All of the tournaments and out of town shenanigans made us family. *#13* for life.

To Margo Cusack and her staff, thank you all for your help during Xavier's journey with cancer. Margo, thank you for calling doctors and helping our family find the best Orthopedic Surgeon at UCSF, Dr. Rosanna Wustrack. Thank you for your arrangements of Xavier's CT, MRI, and bone scan appointments in a timely manner. Our family will be forever grateful for your kindness.

To Xavier's family & friends, including of course those listed above, thank you for taking this journey with Xavier. And to all those who supported, influenced, mentored, and inspired Xavier throughout his life, we thank you. We will forever treasure the stories that came from the beautiful friendships you all shared with Xavier. Keep living the dream. Make each day count. We love you all.

Ron, Rosalie, & Alexander Echon

Xavier: **Till we meet again.**

If you enjoyed this book, please consider checking out some of Xavier's vlogs on YouTube. Thank you.

Thank You https://youtu.be/Gvl-ECEyzSc
The Prologue https://youtu.be/CrG4vvnGsl8
The 10 Percent https://youtu.be/UzPYX12F8Sw
SMC Luminaria Relay for Life https://youtu.be/WVIgB3YXU1I

I Really Do This for You...

In Loving Memory of Xavier Edward Celestino Echon

Sunrises and Sunsets are the same events.
1994 - 2019